THE WEIMAR REPUBLIC

A History of Germany from Ebert to Hitler

LOUIS L. SNYDER

Professor of History
The City University of New York

AN ANVIL ORIGINAL

under the general editorship of

LOUIS L. SNYDER

D. VAN NOSTRAND COMPANY, INC.

PRINCETON, NEW JERSEY

TORONTO   LONDON

NEW YORK

TO
SIDNEY I. POMERANTZ
COLLEAGUE AND TREASURED FRIEND

D. VAN NOSTRAND COMPANY, INC.
120 Alexander St., Princeton, New Jersey (*Principal office*); 24 West 40 St., New York, N.Y.
D. VAN NOSTRAND COMPANY (Canada), LTD.
25 Hollinger Rd., Toronto 16, Canada
D. VAN NOSTRAND COMPANY, LTD.
358, Kensington High Street, London, W.14, England

COPYRIGHT © 1966, BY
LOUIS L. SNYDER
Published simultaneously in Canada by
D. Van Nostrand Company (Canada), Ltd.

PRINTED IN THE UNITED STATES OF AMERICA

PREFACE

The rise and fall of the Weimar Republic is one of the most melancholy political tales of modern times. Defeated in World War I, the German people at long last had a chance to rid themselves of their reactionary past and join the mainstream of Western democracy. Once again, as in 1848, they had an opportunity to break new ground. But the shocking and lamentable denouement of their Republic led straight into the shameful era of Hitler.

It is a depressing story not only for the German people but also for the rest of the world. Had the Weimar Republic succeeded, both Germans and others might well have been spared the horrors of World War II.

The Weimar Republic was sabotaged by its friends and foes alike. The men who tried to make it work were too fainthearted, too hesitant, too reluctant to cast aside the traditions of yesterday. Honest and well-meaning, they made one mistake after another. Inexperienced in handling political power, they tried to share it with unregenerate Prussian militarists and selfish industrial plutocrats, both of whom had only contempt for the Republic and its way of life. It was a coalition inevitably headed for ruin. The Republic was besieged from two sides, by wild nationalists on the Right and by equally fanatical internationalists on the Left. This was nothing new—witness the experience of the Third French Republic which had to steer a course between Communards on the Left and Boulangists and anti-Dreyfusards on the Right. But the men of Weimar took a blundering, tortuous course which satisfied no one. As if this were not enough, they were abandoned by the war victors, who had much to gain from German democracy. Allied statesmen, wearing blinkers, insisted on treating the new Germany as if she were a facsimile of the Bismarckian and Wilhelminian Second

Reich. The result of these interrelated factors was confusion, chaos, and eventually, collapse.

As in all my published work, the production of this volume was facilitated beyond expression by the fine editorial eyes of my wife, who worked diligently on the project from its beginning to its completion.

LOUIS L. SNYDER

New York City
March 1966

TABLE OF CONTENTS

Part 1

THE WEIMAR REPUBLIC

— 1 —

COLLAPSE OF THE MONARCHY:
GERMANY SUES FOR PEACE

The Specter of Defeat. The United States entered World War I on April 6, 1917. Vast manpower and resources were thrown with unexpected speed into the conflict. The scales were tipped in favor of the Allies. But a year later, in the spring of 1918, the German High Command still professed confidence. It pointed to favorable signs. Had not the perfidious Italians been defeated? And had not the Russians withdrawn from the war and signed the Treaty of Brest-Litovsk? Add to these omens of good fortune the defeat of Rumania and the anticipated success of the spring offensive in the West. General Erich Ludendorff, hard-bitten war lord, was certain that he could win a military decision.

Ludendorff's hopes were illusory. His armies had already sustained terrible losses. Reserves thrown into the caldron were either old men unfit for military service or young lads in their teens. Living conditions on the home front were unbearable. Food and clothing had almost vanished; animals were being killed because of lack of fodder; people were dying of influenza; there were strikes and disorders. None would forget that last "turnip winter," when even coffee and cigarettes were made of those hated turnips. The British blockade was working. And the submarine campaign, Germany's last hope, had not brought the expected miracle. No wonder there was defeatist and radical agitation!

11

The great German offensive began on March 21, 1918. Every last bit of military effort went into this final drive to stave off defeat. For a few days there were spectacular results. Yet, it was only the dying gasp of an exhausted army. The offensive pushed with unprecedented fury, but it came to a grinding halt after four months. The Germans were beaten at the Second Battle of the Marne (July 15-August 7, 1918). Ludendorff sensed disaster: August 8, 1918, he wrote in his memoirs, was "the black day of the German army." Defeated on the battlefield, their supplies diminishing to the vanishing point, the home front in a state of disintegration, the German army was on the edge of collapse.

Ludendorff asked Chancellor Georg von Hertling to start negotiations for an armistice to be based on President Wilson's Fourteen Points. The war went on for six more ghastly weeks as the diplomats turned to the task of ending hostilities.

On September 30, 1918, William II accepted the resignation of Chancellor Hertling, who had refused to make any constitutional changes to increase the parliamentary character of the German government. "It is my wish," said the Kaiser when accepting the resignation, "that the German people should participate more effectively than heretofore in the determination of the fate of the Fatherland. It is, therefore, my will that men who enjoy the confidence of the nation should partake extensively of the rights and duties of government." With these words the Emperor took the first step toward the revolution from above as demanded by Ludendorff and other advisers.

Meanwhile, Generals von Hindenburg and Ludendorff cautioned the Emperor that October 1, 1918 was the deadline for commencing armistice negotiations. William selected Prince Max of Baden, his cousin and heir to the grand-ducal throne of Baden, as his new chancellor. It was a shrewd choice. The Prince could be relied upon to stand by the Hohenzollern dynasty in its hour of trial. As heir to the throne of Baden, he had a personal stake in the preservation of the monarchical system in Germany. Moreover, he had a reputation as democratic in outlook, an asset for the stormy days ahead.

The Social Democrats were in a dilemma. Should they support Prince Max's government? Friedrich Ebert, their leader, called for cooperation with the new government. Philipp Scheidemann, the party's second in command, opposed it. Ebert had his way. The new government included two Social Democrats, three Centrists (including Matthias Erzberger), one Progressive, and several members of the old Hertling cabinet. For the first time in the history of the Empire, a government was to be responsible to the *Reichstag*.

On October 1, 1918, the High Command made it clear to the Emperor that "there is no longer any prospect of forcing the enemy to seek peace." Two days later, on October 3, Prince Max sent his first peace note to President Wilson, requesting the American President "to take steps for the restoration of peace." (*See Reading No. 1.*) In his reply Wilson asked whether Prince Max "is speaking merely for the constituted authorities of the Empire who have so far conducted the war." The implication was plain: the President was not inclined to negotiate with William II and was hinting that it might be best for the German people to demand his abdication. Opinion hardened in Washington when word came of the torpedoing on October 12 of a passenger vessel in the Irish Sea. Wilson's stern note of October 14 called for further proof that Prince Max did not represent the "arbitrary power" exercised in Germany. This time the Germans reacted angrily. The exchange of notes continued, but it was clear that there was no alternative to surrender.

On October 26, 1918, Ludendorff resigned his command and was succeeded by General Wilhelm Groener. Prince Max and General Groener now turned to the twin tasks of (1) negotiating for an armistice, and (2) demanding William II's abdication.

The Armistice, November 11, 1918. Early on the morning of November 8, in the midst of a revolutionary situation, Matthias Erzberger, the Centrist leader, arrived in the forest of Compiègne with other members of the German armistice commission. They were received by Ferdinand Foch, the Allied Generalissimo. When the German emissaries asked for conditions, they were told by Foch: "No conditions!" "Do you wish," he asked coldly, "to ask for an armistice? If so, say so." The Germans then asked for an armistice with no conditions attached. Foch read them the main clauses of the armistice note agreed upon by the Allies. Erzberger asked for an immediate cessation of hostilities. Foch declined. He said that hostilities could not be suspended before the signing of the armistice. The German delegation was given seventy-two hours to reply. Erzberger, pointing out the difficulty of communicating with his government, asked for a twenty-four-hour extension. Foch refused again.

The terms laid down by the Allies were severe. (*See Reading No. 5.*) On signing the armistice on the morning of November 11, 1918, the German delegates issued a statement which indicated their dissatisfaction with the terms forced upon them. (*See Reading No. 6.*) They had not been able to obtain milder treatment. For better or for worse the war was over for them.

The Problem of War Guilt. Article 231 of the Treaty of Versailles, the war-guilt clause, held Germany and her allies exclusively responsible for causing the war:

> The Allied and Associated Governments affirm and Germany accepts the responsibility of Germany and her allies for causing all the loss and damage to which the Allied and Associated Governments and their nationals have been subjected as a consequence of the war imposed upon them by the aggression of Germany and her allies.

This controversial clause played directly into the hands of the German war lords. Public indignation, instead of being directed against the military, was turned against the foreigners who placed the onus of guilt on Germany and her allies. Patriotic Germans, regardless of class or party, reacted against this "slur on our honor." A campaign was organized to combat what was called the *"Kriegsschuld-lüge"* ("war-guilt lie"). Popular and scholarly books and articles denied the Allied charge. (*See Reading No. 7.*) The Weimar Republic was to suffer from the controversy, because its representatives had signed the document which contained "that intolerable lie."

The controversy extended to the Allied countries. Historians were split into two sharply divergent groups. One side (Bernadotte Schmitt, H. R. Trevor-Roper) maintained that the war had been the result of German aggression. They held that the German General Staff had wanted war, carefully prepared for it, and devoted forty years to planning it. Admittedly, errors had been made by non-German as well as German statesmen, but these errors were held to be ultimately irrelevant, when compared with the German drive toward war.

After 1919 a group of revisionist historians (Sidney B. Fay, Harry Elmer Barnes) presented the explanation that, while Germany had made some moves that contributed to a war situation, she could not be accused of deliberate plotting to bring about the war. It was false, they said, to paint Germany's prewar record as totally black, for her statesmen had worked more effectively than others to avert the war, and had known that war might jeopardize German progress already attained by peaceful means. Some revisionists substitute this as the order of guilt for immediate responsibility: (1) Serbia; (2) France; (3) Russia; (4) Austria; (5) England; and (6) Germany.

A third approach held that responsibility for the war should be equally distributed, and that the conflict was the fatal result of unresolved economic clashes, diplomatic intrigues, national rivalries, sword rattling, and an unsound psychological concept of security. Those who took this attitude had in mind not the crisis of 1914, but rather the general situation. Serious mistakes of judgment, it was said, were made on all sides during the critical weeks. Most historians saw the milieu as dangerously receptive to seeds of war. Lloyd George explained the catastrophe in these words: "The more one reads of the memoirs and books written in the various countries of what happened before August 1, 1914, the more one realizes that no one at the head of affairs quite meant war. It was something into which they glided, or rather staggered and stumbled."

The Critical Allied Error. In retrospect it seems clear that the triumphant Allies made an error in agreeing to an armistice at a time when the German armies were

intact and all the fighting had taken place on Allied soil.
Not a single square inch of German territory was occupied at the time of the truce. There were no trenches on
German soil. The result was that the German public had
no adequate idea of the disastrous defeat their armies had
suffered on the battlefield. For generations the Germans
had been told that their armies were unconquerable. To
them the military caste was composed of supermen who
knew all about the art of war and who would lead their
men to victory no matter what the odds. It was easy to
maintain a legend of invincibility under such circumstances. By failing to march on Berlin, the Allies threw
away their chance to impress upon the German public
the decisiveness of their defeat.

There was still another error of judgment. President
Wilson made it clear that under no circumstances would
he negotiate with the military masters of Wilhelmian
Germany. He would have nothing to do with the Supreme
Command. This decision had a peculiar result: the German militarists were able to evade the responsibility of
taking part in the all-important act of surrender. They
stepped aside conveniently while political representatives
of the fledgling Republic accepted the odium of defeat.
Thus, in the eyes of the German people, the leaders of
the new democracy, and not the German military, were
thereafter bound up with disgraceful defeat. The Weimar Republic could not survive this reputation.

The Stab-in-the-Back Theory. Almost immediately
German militarists, supported by right-wing politicians
and publicists, projected the theory that the German
army had never been defeated, but had been victimized
by a stab-in-the-back (*Dolchstoss*). (*See Reading No.
8.*) It was a simple and convenient explanation: "subversive" elements at home—pacifists, liberals, Socialists,
Communists, and especially Jews—had so weakened the
domestic front that the military arm could no longer
function. The army collapsed because of the divergent
interests of the men who fought at the front and the
weaklings responsible for the disintegration of the home
front. Propagandists took up the cry. Hitler used it effectively in his blueprint, *Mein Kampf,* and in his struggle

for political power. The Weimar Republic was weakened immeasurably by this myth.

Germany Made Safe for Militarism.   We shall see that the leaders of the revolution threw away an opportunity to create a people's army to strike down the counterrevolution. Instead of making a break with the militaristic past, the republicans hesitated. They allowed army officers, who made no secret of their contempt for the democratic way of life, to retain important commands. Officers of the new *Reichswehr* had no use for their civilian superiors. The new army was inculcated with the ideas and virtues of the old. The military caste, far from being pushed out of the picture, was retained in all its pristine glory. It was another irreversible error made by the men who led the new Republic. For some it was a "revolution lost"—the fearful and anxious *Bürger* abdicated in favor of the discredited military. (*See Reading No. 13.*)

THE REVOLUTION OF 1918

Mutiny at Kiel. While the war was going on, a revolutionary situation was developing on the home front. Since the battle of Jutland, May 31-June 1, 1916, the capital ships of Germany's High Seas Fleet had been bottled up in Kiel and other ports of North Germany. All German naval activities centered around the U-boat weapon, and the crews of other ships were constantly being raided for men able to serve in submarines. The men had little to do beyond maintenance of their craft. They were bored and restless. Some had completed their voluntary four-year enlistment on October 1, 1914, and were now in their eighth or ninth year aboard. In the early days they would have been eager to do their duty for Emperor and Fatherland, but now, with the war going badly, they were anxious only to go home. The long enforced retirement left the men open to intense discussions of radical movements. There was much talk about the Russian sailors on the *Aurora*, anchored in the Neva River near the Winter Palace at Petrograd; nearly a year earlier, on November 6, 1917, sailors from its crew had landed and helped the Red Guards seize and lower the bridges in the city.

In mid-October 1918, Admiral Reinhard Scheer, director of naval operations, decided on a plan which he believed would help the army and redeem the honor of the German navy. He would send the High Seas Fleet on a foray into the North Sea and attack Allied shipping in the seas between Flanders and England. This would lure the British Grand Fleet south from Scapa Flow and result in a naval battle which could snatch victory from defeat. On the evening of October 29, Admiral Hans von Hipper, commander-in-chief, briefed his officers at Kiel on the proposed last-minute action. Members of the crew serving in the officers' mess overheard the admiral's plans and passed the word to their fellows. That night the crews mutinied. On several of the large ships they refused to accept orders. Officers tried to halt the revolt but with no success. By the next morning it became clear that, in view of the behavior of the men, the proposed operation could not be carried out. Ringleaders were arrested and ordered to stand court-martial trial.

The situation in Kiel deteriorated rapidly. There were mass meetings, parades, and demonstrations. Local troops, ordered to arrest the mutineers, instead joined them. Industrial workers called a general strike. By November 3, Kiel was in the hands of the rebels, and their red flag was flying from ships in the harbor. The situation could no longer be controlled. The rebellion spread rapidly along the coast to Hamburg, Bremen, and Lübeck. The success of the mutiny demonstrated that the government was not strong enough to quell revolt.

It has been said that if ever there was a pardonable mutiny, this was it. The sailors at Kiel knew well the superiority of the British fleet. Even if every German ship took one British ship with it to its death, the British navy would still remain a grand fleet and it would still control the seas. In the minds of the sailors of Kiel the code of "death with honor" was fine for a handful of intoxicated officers drinking toasts to death. But had they the right to take with them thousands of good sailors who thus far had done their duty for the Fatherland and were waiting only to go home to their loved ones? Even those immune to revolutionary agitation refused to go along with what they regarded as a futile grandstand play.

Revolution in Bavaria. On November 7, 1918, revolt erupted in Bavaria. The Wittelsbachs, the oldest dynasty in Germany became engulfed in a revolutionary tide flowing through the streets of Munich. Here the red flag was raised. The leader of the Independent Social Democratic party in Munich was Kurt Eisner (1868-1919), journalist and newspaperman, associate editor of the Socialist newspaper *Vorwärts*. Eisner, who had only recently been released from jail, proposed to establish *Räte* (councils) to educate the masses in democracy. He went so far as to give Germany full blame for causing the war. He was opposed not only to the war party but also to the existing political regime.

Eisner's most important ally was war weariness. Bavarians, thoroughly tired of the war, were concerned that the Allies invade Germany from the south through Bavaria. Bavarians always considered themselves the innocent victims of Prussian ambitions, and they had little love for the Prussian way of life. Added to this was the anger of the Bavarian peasants, disgruntled by the nationalization of the agricultural markets. Another factor was the unpopularity of Ludwig III, the Bavarian king. He had refused the regency for the legitimate but mentally ill King Otto and had insisted upon being crowned in Otto's place.

The people of Munich had been considered the most stolid of Germans. Now, moved by Eisner's eloquence, demonstrators in Munich occupied public buildings and seized newspaper plants. They formed workers', soldiers', and peasants' councils in the Russian fashion. Deserted by his troops, who were unwilling to fire on the rebels, Ludwig III fled. A republic was proclaimed. Eisner now declared his opposition to violence. He formed a cabinet, with himself as premier and minister for foreign affairs.

The Abdication of William II. The end of the Wittelsbach dynasty in Bavaria had the effect of a green light all over Germany. Princes in other states followed suit and gave up their thrones. One after another, like a row of dominoes, Germany's major cities succumbed to the tide of revolution: Frankfort, Cologne, Stuttgart, Leipzig. There was little resistance anywhere. The imperial regime collapsed.

As the demonstrations gathered momentum, Prince Max informed William II of what was going on and again implored him to abdicate. As early as October 23, President Wilson had called on Germany to rid herself of her "monarchical autocrats." As long as Germany was ruled by military and monarchical authority, he intimated, she could not expect a negotiated peace but would have to surrender unconditionally. Until this time few Germans had even thought of the possibility of a republic. There had been some discontent with William's flamboyant personality, but little sentiment for abdication. Now it began to dawn on Germans that they might obtain better peace terms if William were no longer the monarch. The question was urgent—the discontinuation of the monarchy was now linked with the survival of the state.

On October 30 Scheidemann sent a letter to the chancellor demanding that the emperor be asked to abdicate. Prince Max asked Scheidemann to withdraw the letter, which he did. On November 1, representatives of the government arrived at Spa and broached the question to William. Supported by Generals von Hindenburg and Groener, William indignantly refused. At that time General Groener suggested that William seek death in the front lines: "He should go to the front not to review troops or to confer decorations but to look for death. He should go to some trench which was under the full blast of war. If he were killed it would be the finest death possible." The emperor found the advice unpalatable.

On the evening of November 6, Prince Max made the difficult decision to go to Spa and inform the emperor that he would have to abdicate in order to save the dynasty from extinction. The Socialist government had sent the chancellor an ultimatum: they would withdraw from the coalition if both emperor and crown prince had not stepped down by noon of November 8. Both Hindenburg and Groener informed William that the army would march home in peace and order under its leaders, but not under the emperor's command. William, still convinced that only he could restore order in Germany, demurred. He would resign as German Emperor but not as King of Prussia.

Finally Prince Max, annoyed by William's indecision, took matters into his own hands in a last effort to save the monarchy. Just before noon on November 9, 1918, he issued this statement to the press:

> The Emperor and King has decided to renounce the throne. The Imperial Chancellor will remain in office until the questions connected with the abdication of the Emperor, the renunciation of the throne of Germany and of Prussia by the Crown Prince, and the establishment of the regency have been settled. He intends to propose to the regent the appointment of Herr Ebert as chancellor and the introduction of a bill providing for the immediate election of a constituent national assembly whose duty it will be to determine the future form of government for the German people.

William II ceased to be sovereign. Abandoned by army, navy, and ministers, he was to become a refugee, forced to seek a home on foreign soil.

— 3 —

BIRTH:
THE ADVENT OF THE REPUBLIC

Ebert Becomes Chancellor. On November 9, 1918, a few minutes after Prince Max had issued his statement regarding William II's renunciation of the throne, Ebert, Scheidemann, and several other Social Democrats called on the chancellor. They demanded that the government be entrusted to men "who enjoy the full confidence of the people." It was too late, they said, to form a regency. Although Prince Max had no constitutional right to appoint his successor, he agreed, with the understanding that a constituent assembly would be convoked. "I commend the German *Reich* to your care," he told Ebert. "For that *Reich*," Ebert replied, "I have lost two sons."

Thus the former saddle maker took over the reins of government. Immediately he issued a manifesto urging the nation to remain tranquil so that the government could take steps to cope with the serious food shortage. (*See Reading No. 2.*) The transfer of authority to the Social Democrats did not automatically mean the end of monarchy in Germany. At this moment Ebert had no idea of forming a republic. Both he and Prince Max were willing to await the decision of a democratically elected constituent assembly, which would make the final decision about the new form of government. Prince Max was motivated by royalist sentiment. He was convinced that with Ebert as chancellor there was a hope that the monarchy could be retained. Ebert would make a satisfactory caretaker. And better Ebert than Karl Liebknecht and the Bolsheviks!

Proclamation of the German Republic. Two days earlier, on November 7, 1918, Kurt Eisner had proclaimed a republic in Bavaria. Revolutionary zeal spread to Berlin. On the morning of November 9, while Prince Max was turning the government over to Ebert, great crowds swarmed through the streets and headed toward the center of the city. Recalcitrant troops refused to obey commands. Some even approached their officers and pulled off insignia of rank. The mob was in an ugly mood.

After issuing his manifesto, Ebert, together with his colleagues, returned to the *Reichstag* building and sat down to a meager lunch. Outside in the square a great crowd was shouting and singing. Ebert, Scheidemann, and other members of the executive committee of the Majority Socialists were in a quandary. Word came that less than a mile away, in the *Lustgarten*, the leaders of the Independent Socialists were haranguing another crowd. Liebknecht and the Spartacists were about to proclaim a soviet republic. Ebert and Scheidemann agreed that they would have to go beyond the limits that they had set for themselves. It was a decisive moment.

Several workers and soldiers ran into the dining hall and demanded that Scheidemann address the crowd gathered outside. Something had to be done at once to head off the Bolsheviks. Scheidemann needed no urging. He rushed to the balcony of the *Reichstag* and there, at two o'clock, proclaimed the German Republic. (*See Reading No. 3.*) It is not clear whether Scheidemann deliberately decided to act without consulting his colleagues, or whether he was carried away by the enthusiasm of the moment.

Happy in the belief that he had stopped the Bolshevik drive for power, Scheidemann returned to the dining room only to find a horrified and angry Ebert. "You have no right to proclaim the Republic," Ebert informed him. "What becomes of Germany—whether she becomes a republic or something else— must be decided by a constituent assembly." But it was too late. Scheidemann's words could not be retracted. Ebert decided to make the best of the situation. He accepted the action of his impulsive colleague as a *fait accompli* and reconciled himself to it. Thus, in this highly informal, almost accidental

manner, without barricades or bloodshed in the streets,
the Weimar Republic came into existence.

On that same memorable day, November 9, 1918, William II, ensconced at Spa, reiterated his determination to
remain at his post as King of Prussia. In great agitation
he called upon his generals to blast the rebellious Socialists out of Berlin. But his military advisers made it clear
to him that it was impossible to lead the army into the
capital. Hindenburg informed him that his life was not
safe at Spa and insisted that he leave Germany as soon
as possible. In the late afternoon, with great reluctance,
William ordered his train pulled to the Dutch border.
He asked for and obtained asylum from Wilhelmina,
queen of the Netherlands. The next morning he was in
Holland.

It was not until November 28, 1918 that William II
formally renounced his throne. (*See Reading No. 9.*)
The last of the Hohenzollerns, he retired to Doorn, where
he spent his remaining twenty-three years in exile. The
"woodchopper of Doorn" presided over the remnant of
his court, wrote an apologia for his life, and occupied
his mind with the study of archaeology. He died in May
1941.

Formation of the Provisional Government. The Republic was proclaimed in the midst of chaos. Mobs surged
through the streets of Berlin either hailing the new government or demanding its abolition. Loudest was the
Bolshevik minority which looked to Moscow for inspiration. Had not the Russian minority, armed and activistic,
won its way to power? Ebert's government was tottering
from the moment of its inception.

Within an hour after assuming the chancellorship,
Ebert invited the Independents to join the Majority Socialists in forming a new cabinet. This was no idle gesture.
Ebert knew well that his party was not strong enough to
govern alone. A coalition with the Independents would
give him a fairly broad base. True, his own party represented the greater part of the German workers, but the
Independents, pitched farther to the Left, spoke for the
active Berlin proletariat. They were the spearhead of the
revolution. And they were busily creating workers' councils not only in Berlin but throughout the country. Within

a few days they would probably be in a position to demand all power for the soviets.

In response to Ebert's request the Independents asked for time to talk the matter over. The intra-party discussion immediately revealed a sharp difference of opinion. The Right-wingers, led by Wilhelm Dittmann, argued in favor of collaboration with the Majority Socialists. The Left-wingers, led by Emil Barth, a vociferous metal worker who represented the radical Shop Stewards and the workers' and soldiers' soviet in Berlin, denounced Ebert and Scheidemann as traitors to the cause of socialism, and refused any negotiations with them. Barth was supported by Liebknecht, who demanded the transfer of power to the workers' and soldiers' councils.

The Right-wingers wanted socialism, not sovietism. But they were forced to yield on the critical point of collaboration. The Left-wingers agreed on a short-term cooperation. Late in the afternoon of November 9, 1918, the Independents sent Ebert a list of demands. Germany, they said, would have to be a "social republic." There were three stipulations: (1) the cabinet ministers must be only Socialists; (2) all political power was to be in the hands of the councils; and (3) the constituent assembly was not to be called until "the revolution was consolidated." The Independents would collaborate for not more than three days—just long enough to conclude an armistice with the Allies.

The Majority Socialists replied that evening. They, too, wanted a "social republic," but the German people would have to decide that. As for all power for the councils, this was contrary to the principles of the Social Democratic party, and it meant class dictatorship. This demand was rejected. The time-limit was nonsense: the two Socialist parties had to cooperate at least until the convocation of the constituent assembly.

The Independents gave their response the next morning, November 10, 1918. They insisted upon the first two of their original demands—the cabinet ministers must be Socialists only, and all political power was to be in the hands of the councils. They lifted the time limit on their participation in the government—the only concession. The Majority Socialists, still annoyed by the two stipulations, nevertheless felt the urgency of setting up a government as quickly as possible. They capitulated and accepted the stipulations of the Independents.

A six-man Council of People's Representatives was formed (the name "cabinet" was rejected as a "bourgeois term"). The Majority Socialists were represented by Ebert, Scheidemann, and Otto Landsberg. The Independents named Dittmann, Haase, and Barth. With the exception of Barth, all were experienced members of the *Reichstag*. Landsberg and Haase were able lawyers. Liebknecht, still calling for a soviet government, declined to take any part in the regime.

Late in the afternoon of that same day, November 10, 1918, the workers' and soldiers' council of Berlin assembled to elect an executive committee. Ebert announced that the new government representing both Socialist parties had been formed. The assembly gave its sanction to the Council. Then it turned to the business of electing the committee. The Spartacists and Shop Stewards suddenly proposed the election of a committee composed only of radicals. Delegates of the soldiers' councils objected that the army was not Marxist and that it should have equal representation with the workers. The soldiers won their point: a committee was set up consisting of twelve soldiers and twelve workers (the latter representing both Majority Socialists and Independents). Liebknecht and Rosa Luxemburg, denouncing the Majority Socialists, refused to serve. This victory by the soldiers' council was the first indication that the German revolution was departing from the Russian pattern.

On November 12, 1918, the Ebert Council issued a proclamation to describe the aims of the new regime. (*See Reading No. 4.*) The preamble was a concession to the Independents: "The government created by the Revolution, the policy of which is purely Socialist, is setting itself the task of implementing the Socialistic program." But this document, notable as it was, did not promulgate any Socialist measures. It restored freedom of speech, press, and assembly, granted amnesty to political offenders, and promised socio-political reforms. It expressed all the ideas that had been supported by Socialists and liberals for many years in Germany. It reflected

Ebert's belief in orderly, peaceful progress rather than violence and bloodshed. Ebert wanted socialism as the ultimate goal, but he believed that it had to come slowly, through the ballot box. To the Left-wing Independents, however, the proclamation was nothing more than an expression of outmoded bourgeois ideals. It was meaningless, they contended, without social democracy.

Revival of the Militaristocrats: the Ebert-Groener Deal.   For Ebert the most important thing in the world was the preservation of the fledgling Republic. He understood his own dangerous position: he had to protect the government from extremist attacks from both Left and Right. And the Majority Socialists had no armed force which could perform this vital task. The Independents were demanding the formation at once of a citizens' militia. But Ebert, thoroughly familiar with the Russian Revolutions of 1917, wanted no vanguards of Bolshevism in Germany.

On November 10, 1918, Ebert, without informing his colleagues, got in touch by telephone with the Supreme Command at its headquarters in Spa. He proposed an understanding with General Groener that the country be saved by the army from Bolshevism and civil war. Groener was receptive to the idea. It meant a chance to "combat the revolution" and to maintain the role of the military in German affairs. Groener had no difficulty in persuading Hindenburg, who hated the new workers' and soldiers' councils, to go along. Groener informed Ebert that Hindenburg would remain at the head of the Supreme Command and would be at Ebert's disposal. As a *quid pro quo,* the government would support the officers' corps.

This deal resulted in one of the most harrowing controversies of the German revolution. While it sealed the doom of German Bolshevism, it delivered the Republic into the hands of the militaristocrats. This was to have fateful consequences. After this alliance, Ebert could never attempt the task of creating a republican army. Germany had been made safe for militarism again. There would be fateful consequences.

The *Freikorps*: Gravediggers of the Republic.   The struggle for power was not yet ended. Millions of demobilized soldiers were coming home as the defeated army melted away. Some returned to jobs, others wandered aimlessly or joined in the discussions held by soldiers' councils. Tough agitators tried to win the people to their point of view. Bullets whistled through the streets of Berlin. Armed bands occupied the palace and newspaper offices, and even threatened the chancellery.

On the Left, radicals led by Liebknecht and Luxemburg deemed the moment ripe for extending the revolution to its soviet goal. On the Right, semiorganized units arose to fight the battle of the streets against the radicals. In 1813 a Major Lützow had organized the first *Freikorps* (volunteer corps) as the kernel of an army dedicated to liberating Germans from Napoleon. Now a new *Freikorps* of volunteers attracted officers, military adventurers, demobilized soldiers, fanatical nationalists, and unemployed youths. These Rightists, motivated by the stab-in-the-back theory, blamed Socialists and Jews for Germany's plight. They would eliminate the "traitors to the Fatherland." At first Hindenburg and the other generals encouraged the formation of *Freikorps* units, until the bestial behavior of the volunteers made them obnoxious to the old military clique.

Civil War in Germany. The marriage of convenience between the Majority Socialists and the Independents could not and did not last. Tension between the rival camps rose during November and early December of 1918. The Majority Socialists, unprepared for power, had been surprised by the sudden collapse of the imperial regime. Beset by defeat, starvation, and economic troubles, they had to bear the responsibility for national reconstruction in perilous times. It was not an easy or simple task.

Ebert and the Majority Socialists were worried about the Spartacist call for a sovietized *Reich*. Founded in 1917, the *Spartakusbund* was named after Spartacus, the Roman gladiator who in 83 B.C. urged his fellow slaves to revolt. Its leaders were Karl Liebknecht (1871-1919), [son of the German Socialist Wilhelm Liebknecht], and Rosa Luxemburg (1870-1919). Karl Liebknecht's antimilitarism and radicalism had led to his expulsion from the *Reichstag* in 1916. Sentenced to four years of penal servitude for high treason, he was released in October 1918. Rosa Luxemburg, of Polish descent, had acquired German nationality by marrying a German workman. A veteran of the Russian uprising of 1905, she was imprisoned during World War I and released in 1918. She joined Liebknecht as co-editor of the *Rote Fahne*.

Both Liebknecht and Luxemburg considered Ebert as hopelessly bourgeois. They called for immediate sovietization of Germany and for the world revolution. (*See Reading No. 10.*) They borrowed their theme from Soviet Russia: "All power—legislative, executive, and judicial—to the workers' and soldiers' soviets!" Both enjoyed enormous popularity among the Berlin radicals.

The tension between the Majority Socialists and their proletarian rivals led to bloodshed on December 6, 1918. A crowd of unarmed Spartacists, alarmed by rumors of counterrevolution, demonstrated on the streets of Berlin. Troops intercepted them, and in the excitement of the moment, opened fire. Several participants were killed and many more wounded. Spartacist leaders used this incident to fan the emotions of their followers.

On December 16, 1918, a congress of workers' and soldiers' councils assembled in the Prussian House of Deputies in Berlin. The majority of the delegates supported Ebert and Scheidemann and the Majority Socialists. Liebknecht and Luxemburg, counting on this meeting to insure the triumph of Sovietism in Germany, were astonished when the assembly voted overwhelmingly against seating them. A group of Spartacists thereupon forced their way into the hall and demanded the end of Ebert's government, supreme power for the soviets, the formation of a Red Army, and the world revolution. The next day Emil Barth, announcing that his patience was at an end, denounced Ebert for establishing "treasonable relations with the military camarilla." He proposed that the officers' corps be abolished. The meetings degenerated into a series of tongue-lashings by all sides. The congress ended on a note of disunity, but advanced the date of the elections for the national constituent assembly from February 16 to January 19, 1919.

Because of his understanding with General Groener, Ebert had sizable military forces at his disposal. Meanwhile, 3000 sailors belonging to the People's Naval Division, were causing a serious problem in the former royal palace in Berlin. When the government ordered them to move out, the sailors refused. On December 23, 1918, they made their way to the chancellery and ordered that no one go in or out. Ebert, using a secret telephone line, called the regular army troops.

Early the next morning, December 24, an army division opened fire on the palace. After two hours of fighting an agreement was reached: the sailors consented to withdraw from the palace and the government promised to remove the unpopular city commander. Many Berliners were angered by the shooting of republican sailors by anti-republican troops under the command of the old militarists. Three days later, the Independents—Haase, Dittmann, and Barth—announced their resignation from the Council of People's Representatives. Their places were taken by Majority Socialists. The latter, who preferred to be called Social Democrats, now had full political authority.

On December 30, 1918, a national conference of the Spartacists opened in Berlin. Sparked by Liebknecht and Luxemburg, the Spartacists repudiated the Independents, "who had forfeited their right to be called the standard bearers of the revolutionary masses." This repudiation ended the formal tie between the two Left-wing factions. From this time on, the Spartacists were to call themselves the Communist party of Germany. Further discussion at the conference revealed another serious difference inside the party. Luxemburg argued that the revolutionary movement was as yet too weak to undertake a *putsch* against the Ebert government. Even Liebknecht was convinced by this reasoning. But the majority of the delegates voted for an immediate revolt.

Events played into the hands of the *putschists*. When the Independents withdrew from his cabinet, Ebert tried to force the resignation of Berlin's chief of police, Emil Eichhorn. The Independents accepted the challenge and ordered Eichhorn to remain at his post. The Communists gave their support. On January 5, 1919, the two radical parties issued a manifesto summoning the people of Berlin to a "mighty demonstration." (*See Reading No. 11.*)

Immediately a huge throng clogged the streets of Berlin. The next day both rival camps demonstrated in the streets. The issue had come to a head.

Noske: Bloodhound of the Revolution. When the Independents seceded from Ebert's cabinet, Gustave Noske (1868-1946), a former basket weaver, newspaper editor, and trade-union leader, was named minister of war. In late October 1918, at the time of the Kiel mutiny, he was selected to represent the government in talks with the sailors. He performed this task well: he listened to the demands of the mutineers and in a short time order was restored. Ebert picked Noske to win the battle of the streets against the Communists. Noske was convinced that his actions were predetermined by the deadly aims of the Spartacists. "Somebody," he said, "has to be the bloodhound. I will not shirk the responsibility."

The fighting began on a large scale on January 11, 1919, under Noske's direction. He did not hesitate to use *Freikorps* volunteers as well as regular army men. For four days he attacked Bolshevik strongholds in Berlin. Hundreds of radicals were killed in the action. Some were executed, others were ruthlessly manhandled. Noske decided to teach them a lesson they would never forget. By January 15 the operation was successful. The German military machine was back in power. (*See Reading No. 12.*)

During "Spartacus Week" in Berlin, Noske stepped straight into a historical controversy. He was defended by those who thought the democratic Ebert government worth saving. Winston Churchill judged him kindly: "A son of the people, amid universal confusion, [Noske] acted without fear in a public cause." But Noske's enemies denounced him as "the saboteur-in-chief of the revolution" and as an evil man who was "determined to drown the revolution in blood."

Murder of Liebknecht and Luxemburg. Karl Liebknecht and Rosa Luxemburg, the Communist leaders, were able to hide for several days in the midst of the carnage. On January 15, 1919, both were arrested and charged with complicity in the disturbances. While being conveyed to Moabit prison, the two were attacked by former cavalry officers. Liebknecht was killed "while seeking to escape," and Luxemburg was beaten so badly that she died a few hours later. Her body was cast into the *Landwehrkanal*, from which it was recovered on May 31.

There is some confusion as to whether or not the two Communists were slain by reactionary freebooters. It is probable that Luxemburg was killed by an angered mob. The murders were welcomed by many Berliners as a relief from terrible danger; few citizens were interested in justice in those days. Erich Eyck delivered this judgment: "While it is true that we all have experienced too much violence at the hands of Liebknecht's and Luxemburg's friends to be able to feel a strong sense of revulsion at the manner of their death, nevertheless a curse clung to this wretched deed: by helping destroy distaste for violence and respect for human lives in Germany it helped teach the nation to accept brutal and bloody force as a legitimate tool of domestic politics."

Although the radicals had suffered crushing blows, they were not yet ready to capitulate. While most workers had not given their support to the Spartacists, they could not understand why the Socialist government, supposedly on their side, had used army troops and reactionary *Freikorps* ruffians to fire on the workers. The *Freikorps* volunteers enjoyed the work of repression: they felt they were striking blows at both Bolsheviks and the government. In March 1919 came another bloody incident. Noske ordered that anyone combating the government was to be shot if captured. Some 1,200 workers were killed as a result of this command.

The rift between the Social Democrats and the revolutionary workers was never healed. To the proletarian radicals, the Social Democrats were "Cossacks" and agents of the bourgeoisie. To moderate Socialists, the Communist tactics indicated what might be expected in the future from the Bolsheviks. The hatred engendered in the Spartacist uprising helped pave the way for the rise of Hitler. Had the Social Democrats and Communists worked together in the critical days of early 1933, they might have eliminated the Nazi threat. But both sides refused, each preferring to take its chances with Hitler. It was a fatal mistake.

Liquidation of the Communist Republic in Bavaria. The drama of civil war now shifted to Munich. The Bavarian elections of January 12, 1919 resulted in defeat for Kurt Eisner. Although at first he refused to step down, Eisner resigned on February 21. As he was walking on the street on his way to open the Bavarian *Landtag,* he was shot and killed by Count Anton Arco-Valley, a twenty-two-year-old aristocratic counterrevolutionary. It was a senseless crime: Eisner had already been defeated.

The assassination of Eisner set off a wave of revolt throughout Bavaria. Workers formed a revolutionary Central Council. On April 4, 1919, the Communist-controlled Council forbade the *Landtag* to meet again, and three days later proclaimed a Republic of Soviets. The Communist Republic refused to collaborate at all with "the despicable Ebert-Scheidemann-Noske-Erzberger regime." The legitimate Bavarian government fled to Bamberg. The revolutionaries quickly showed that they were incapable of governing. In seeking to purge their opponents, they paved the way for their own extinction. In the civil war which followed there were atrocities on both sides. In late April 1919, Noske's troops from Berlin converged on Munich and liquidated the soviet government and its leaders. Anti-Bolshevik sentiment was so strong that many unfortunate persons were executed who had nothing to do with the Communist regime.

Whatever revolutionary urge the Bavarians had was swept away by the excesses of the radicals. Now the people had had enough of martial law and executions. They were inclined to blame the radicals more than the Rightists. Thousands turned to associations that promised to save them from Bolshevism. From then on Munich became the center of conservatism and reactionary extremism. *Freikorps* leaders began to plot assassinations of prominent republicans. Nazism was born in this atmosphere of hatred. (*See Reading No. 13.*)

— 4 —

FRAMEWORK:
THE WEIMAR CONSTITUTION

The Weimar Constituent Assembly. The crushing
of the Berlin radicals in January 1919 opened the way
for elections to the National Constituent Assembly. More
than 30 million went to the polls on January 19, 1919.
All persons above the age of twenty were allowed to
vote. For the first time in German history women were
given the franchise. An elaborate system of proportional
representation was used to equate the division of seats
with the will of the voters. The results were as follows:

	Votes	*Seats*
Majority Socialists	11,509,100	163
Centrists	5,980,200	91
Democratic Party	5,641,800	75
Nationalists	3,121,500	44
Independents	2,317,300	22
People's Party	1,345,600	19
Miscellaneous	484,800	7

The vote indicated that the people agreed basically
with the political developments that had taken place since
November. The Majority Socialists made the best showing. Of the 421 seats, the Socialist parties won only 185
(the Majority Socialists 163 and the Independent Socialists just 22). It was obvious that only a diminishing part
of the electorate favored the idea of a dictatorship of the
proletariat and a system of soviets. Just as clearly, the

people were reluctant to return to a monarchy: the Nationalists, outright advocates of royalty, won only 44 seats, while the People's Party, which wanted to keep the question open, had only 19. The Assembly represented neither the old ruling groups, nor big business, nor the extreme revolutionaries. Its major emphasis was on middle-class interests, but it leaned toward democratic socialism. Its center of gravity was just left of center.

On February 3, 1919, the Central Council of the Workers' and Soldiers' Soviets formally transferred its powers to the National Constituent Assembly. Three days later the Assembly convened in the Thuringian city of Weimar. The city was selected for two reasons, one political and the second psychological. First, it was some distance from Berlin, which harbored the radical proletariat and which bore the scars of street fighting. Second, the government wanted the people as well as their Allied judges to know that the new Germany had returned to the classical-humanistic Weimar of Goethe and Schiller rather than to the militaristic Potsdam of Frederick the Great and Bismarck.

The first business at hand was the election of a provisional president of the *Reich*. Ebert received 277 votes out of the 379 cast. Conservatives were distressed by the sight of a former harness maker at the head of the *Reich*, but others recognized in Ebert an honest, decent patriot, a hard-working political leader, and an able representative of German trade unionism. In his acceptance speech Ebert promised that he would regard himself as the representative of the entire German people. At the same time he pointed out that he was a son of the working class. But he intimated to Communists and Independents that he would fight any attempt to win power by violence.

Ebert chose as chancellor his right-hand man, Philipp Scheidemann. Because no party had received an absolute majority, Scheidemann had to form a coalition cabinet. The most effective combination under the circumstances seemed to be a government made up of Majority Socialists, Democrats, and Centrists, which came to be known as the Weimar Coalition. German Nationalists were not included in the cabinet because their inclusion

would have been taken by the Allies as a challenge. In
this way the conservatives enjoyed the political advantage
of escaping formal responsibility for the task of peace-
making.

Gustave Noske stayed on as minister of war. Count
Brockdorff-Rantzau, an experienced diplomat without
party affiliation, was appointed foreign minister. Hugo
Preuss, the leading Democrat, was made minister of the
interior. The Center Party was represented by Matthias
Erzberger as minister of finance, Johannes Bell as colonial minister, and the trade-union leader Johann Giesberts
as postmaster-general. This alliance of factions represented three-fourths of the Assembly. Despite denuncia-
tory speeches from both Right and Left, the cabinet received a vote of confidence.

The government announced its aims: peace in accordance with Wilson's Fourteen Points; admission of Germany to the League of Nations; disarmament of all nations; compulsory arbitration of international disputes;
educational opportunities for all Germans; a democratic
army; collective bargaining; freedom of speech, press,
religion, learning, and art.

Versailles: The Establishment of Peace. The first
and basic task of the government was the making of
peace. In April 1919 it set a number of instructions to be
used by its representatives at the Versailles Peace Conference. The Wilsonian program must be binding to both
sides. Germany must not be hampered politically, economically, or militarily. Her colonies must be returned.
There should be no unilateral disarmament. Armed with
these instructions, the German delegation, under the
leadership of Brockdorff-Rantzau, came to Versailles on
April 29, 1919. It learned immediately that the Allies
had no intention of discussing matters. The Germans
had to make all observations in writing. They were
bluntly handed the terms on May 7. (*See Reading No.
14.*)

The terms of the treaty were severe. (*See Reading No.
16.*) Germany was to lose an eighth of her land area,
some 6,500,000 people, all her colonies, and virtually
all her investments abroad. She was required to relin-
quish Alsace and Lorraine to France; Eupen, Malmédy,

and Moresnet to Belgium; parts of Upper Silesia to Czechoslovakia and Poland; northern Schleswig to Denmark; West Prussia and Posen to Poland; Danzig to the League of Nations under mandate; Memel to the Allies; Kiao-chau to Japan; and her remaining colonies to the major powers as mandates of the League of Nations.

Germany was required to submit to Allied occupation of the Rhineland with provisions for gradual retirement. The German army was limited to 100,000 men, and conscription was abolished. The German navy was limited to six battleships, six light cruisers, twelve destroyers, and twelve torpedo boats, and no submarines were permitted. The manufacture of munitions was restricted, the use of poison gas was prohibited, and fortifications along the North and Baltic Seas were ordered demolished. The German General Staff was abolished. William II and other leaders were to be tried before Allied tribunals as violators of international peace.

From the German point of view the crowning insult of all was the war-guilt clause, Article 231, which held Germany and her allies responsible for causing all the loss and damage of the war. This article had been inserted in the treaty by the Allies to justify their claim for the damage wrought by Germany.

The German peace delegates were horrified by the Allied terms. There was an explosion of wrath throughout Germany when the stipulations became known. Newspaper columns were filled with expressions of outrage. Mass meetings were called to protest the proceedings at Versailles. The German government informed the peace delegation to tell the Allies that their terms were "unfulfillable, unbearable, and ruinous." It issued a proclamation denouncing the treaty and holding that it violated the pre-armistice agreement.

In the next several weeks the German delegation strove mightily to obtain some modification of the peace terms. Its members denied angrily that Germany was solely responsible for the war. Again and again they came back to the argument that the terms flatly contradicted Wilson's Fourteen Points, "accepted by both sides as a basis for peace." They resented the surrender of all

Germany's colonies when the fifth of the Fourteen Points had promised "a free, open-minded, and absolutely impartial adjustment of all colonial claims." They objected to the idea of unilateral disarmament, and especially to the provisions concerning the so-called "war criminals."

The attitude of the Allies stiffened. In a note of June 16, 1919, they gave their "last word" and demanded an answer within five days. The Germans obtained a forty-eight hour extension. The government in Berlin wavered. There was much debate, much soul searching. On June 19 the cabinet submitted its resignation after six ministers voted for acceptance of the treaty and eight for its rejection. Ebert stayed at his post, but Scheidemann resigned in protest, to be succeeded by Gustav Bauer and a new cabinet. On June 23, 1919, four hours before the expiration of the ultimatum, the National Assembly agreed to accept the treaty by a vote of 237 for, 138 against, and 5 abstentions. Two hours later a note was sent to Versailles agreeing to accept and sign the peace treaty "imposed by the Allied and Associated governments." (*See Reading No. 15.*)

On June 28, 1919, the fifth anniversary of the assassination of the Austrian Archduke Francis Ferdinand at Sarajevo, the German delegation signed the treaty. The ceremony took place in the Hall of Mirrors at Versailles, where, forty-eight years earlier, the Second German Empire had been proclaimed. That same day a German newspaper appeared with a mourning band on its front page, announcing that "today German honor is dragged to the grave," and calling for vengeance. (*See Reading No. 17.*) Others called it "a black day in our history."

German historians, almost without exception, argued that the peace treaty was a symbol of all that was wrong in the postwar world. Their case was bolstered in 1920 by the publication of John Maynard Keynes' *Economic Consequences of the Peace,* in which the treaty was denounced as "an apparatus of self-deception." In Keynes' view its provisions were "dishonorable, injurious, abhorrent, and detestable." They revealed "imbecile greed," "oppression and rapine." They "reduced Germany to servitude." Others attacked the Keynes interpretation as pessimistic, unreasonable, and unfair. Far from establishing a Carthaginian peace, it was said, the treaty was as intelligent a one as could be devised in an explosive situation. This view held that the peace terms were proper, and that they could have been carried out had the Germans a real desire to live in peace with their neighbors. The argument continues to the present day.

There is little doubt, however, that the Treaty of Versailles dealt a serious blow to the Weimar Republic. In their rush to weaken Germany the Allies overlooked the fact that the Weimar coalition, their natural ally, was being placed in an intolerable and untenable position. Instead of helping to make Germany safe for democracy, the Allies burdened the fledgling Republic with the onus of war guilt. The peace treaty strengthened the reactionaries by giving them a propaganda weapon of inestimable value.

Making the Constitution. The second major problem of the National Assembly was to draft a constitution. Dr. Hugo Preuss, a distinguished liberal jurist, was appointed head of a committee whose membership was based proportionately on the strength of the parties in the Assembly. These legal experts labored zealously, but the final draft was largely the work of Preuss.

There were many problems to be solved. A key issue was centralism versus federalism. Once again there arose the age-old ogre of German particularism, that accent on states' rights that had burdened German history for generations. The South German states objected to the formation of an *Einheitsstaat,* a centralized state. Bavaria had no intention of surrendering rights and privileges which she had enjoyed for centuries. Preuss himself wanted to break down the artificial boundaries of the historic German states and establish a centralized government controlled from Berlin. But once more the old units were able to maintain their identity.

It was a difficult task to push through an entirely new parliamentary system. In the course of debate Preuss issued a fateful warning:

One finds suspicions everywhere. Germans cannot shake off their old political timidity and their deference to the authoritarian state. They do not understand that the new government must be blood of their blood, flesh of their flesh, that their trusted representatives will have to be an integral part of it. Their constant worry is: how can we best keep our constituted representatives so shackled that they will be unable to do anything?

Preuss had little interest in social and economic questions. He left these problems for discussion following submission of the first draft of the constitution. To satisfy the Socialists a section had to be included concerning economic and labor problems. But the Socialist program as a whole was gradually whittled down.

Preuss's draft of the constitution was laid before the Assembly on February 24, 1919. Within ten days, after considerable discussion, the draft was passed at its first reading. But a constitutional committee was ordered to consider it point by point and report back to the Assembly. The committee met for three and a half months and submitted a final draft. This was passed on July 31, 1919 by a vote of 262 to 75. The constitution was promulgated on August 11, 1919.

The Weimar Constitution. The Weimar constitution was a letter-perfect document embodying the best features of the British Bill of Rights, the French Declaration of the Rights of Man and the Citizen, and the first Ten Amendments of the American constitution. (*See Reading No. 18.*) Although the form of government was a republic, it was designated as the German *Reich* and not the German Republic. (Until World War I the term "*Reich*" was considered to mean "Empire"; now it took on the meaning of "Nation" or "Federation.") Retention of the name "*Reich*" indicated the desire of the majority of the Assembly to regard the new regime as continuing the tradition of the older Germany rather than breaking sharply with the past.

Looking back to the days of 1848, the makers of the constitution incorporated into their document the freedoms that had been sought in that revolutionary year. All Germans were declared equal before the law. They were free to travel or to emigrate from Germany. Freedom of speech was guaranteed and there would be no censorship. Communications and the home were guaranteed as sacred. Citizens under arrest had to be informed within twenty-four hours of the nature of the charges. The constitution went into detail not only on the critical question of civil rights but also on economic, social, and religious matters. Compulsory education was regarded as an obligation of the state. Germans were guaranteed full religious freedom.

There were strong feelings about the national colors. One side wanted the black, white, and red associated with the Bismarckian state. The other side insisted on the black, red, and gold of the 1848 days. There was a compromise: the national colors were declared to be black, red, and gold, but the merchant flag was to be black, white, and red with the national colors in the upper inside corner.

The president of the *Reich* was to be chosen by the direct election of the people, for a term of seven years with the possibility of re-election. Any German at least thirty-five years of age was eligible for the office. Later legislation provided that, if no candidate received a majority of all votes cast in an election for the presidency, a second election would be decided by a plurality of the votes cast. President Ebert's provisional title of president was confirmed without the formality of a national election.

Invested with executive authority, the president had considerably less power than the emperor had previously held. All his orders had to be countersigned by the chancellor. He took on a legislative function in the sense that, if he declined to enact a law within three months of its passage by the *Reichstag*, he could call for a referendum of the people on the matter. He had the power to dissolve the *Reichstag* and call for new elections. He appointed the chancellor, who, together with his cabinet, governed the country.

Legislative power was vested in a bicameral body. Members of the lower house, the *Reichstag*, were to be elected for a maximum of four years by secret, universal suffrage and according to proportional representation. The system of proportional representation, designed to give a voice to all political views, had the disadvantage of encouraging many splinter parties. The *Reichstag* was the supreme expression of the popular will and the sovereign legislative power. It initiated and enacted laws, subject to a suspensive veto. The cabinet was responsible to the *Reichstag*.

The *Reichsrat*, the upper house, represented the German states (*Länder*). Each state was to have at least one member in the *Reichsrat*. The memory of prewar Prussian control of the *Bundesrat* had led to a stipulation that no one state could control more than two-fifths of the council. The *Reichsrat* could initiate legislation together with the cabinet. If it disapproved a measure passed by the *Reichstag*, it could return the bill to that body; the latter could override the veto by a two-thirds vote. The *Reichsrat* was to enjoy less power than it had in the Bismarckian *Reich*.

Loophole: Article 48.   Article 48 turned out to be the most controversial item of the constitution. This provided that if any *Land* did not live up to its constitutional obligations, the president could force it to do so by use of the armed forces. It stated further: "In the event that the public order and security are seriously disturbed or endangered, the *Reich* President may take the measures necessary for their restoration, intervening, if necessary, with the aid of the armed forces." For this purpose he could abrogate temporarily, wholly, or in part, the fundamental principles laid down in several articles of the constitution. These included Article 114 (freedom of the individual); Article 115 (freedom of residence); Article 117 (secrecy of postal, telegraph, and telephone communications); Article 118 (freedom of expression); Article 123 (freedom of assembly); Article 124 (freedom of organization); and Article 153 (personal property guarantee). There was a safeguard in that the president was supposed to report his use of Article 48 immediately to the *Reichstag*, which could rescind his action. However, the *Reichstag* would need a working majority to make this safeguard effective.

Critics have wondered how it was that constitutional experts, who were producing one of the most advanced democratic documents in history, could have fallen into the trap of including Article 48. This provision would later play a critical role in the history of the Republic. Certainly its framers did not intend to put into the hands of the president the powers later assumed by President Hindenburg. Article 48 provided the perfect opening wedge for weapons to destroy the Republic. It was abused in such a way that it led to the "legal" dictatorship of Adolf Hitler. The men who made the constitution, operating in times of political instability, were anxious to provide for effective control of both Right and Left. But what they did, perhaps unwittingly, was to provide the enemies of the constitution with a deadly flaw which could be used to squeeze the life out of the Republic. Article 48 is rightly called "the suicide clause."

A Compromise Document. The Weimar constitution, the formulation of a stalemate, was a compromise document which accepted the outer forms of democracy, but breathed no democratic life into the structure that had been created. It satisfied no political party: designed to please all, it gratified none. The Majority Socialists had not been able to achieve even their minimum program. The Independent Socialists regarded the constitution simply as a betrayal of the people. The Democrats considered its language far too proletarian and charged that it had loopholes which would lead to radical experimentation. The Centrists denounced it for its attention to secular ideas. The Nationalists damned it as an inexcusable break with Germany's traditional past; they wanted nothing to do with an opening clause stating: "The German Reich is a Republic. Political authority emanates from the people."

Preuss's original draft of the constitution had called for the fragmentation of Prussia into several smaller states. But the final draft left Prussia territorially intact. Once more Prussia had survived a crisis. Throughout her history she had shown a persistent will to overcome adverse circumstances. True, the new constitution shattered Prussian executive authority, including her key position in the *Reichsrat*. But because of her size Prussia still retained an important influence in German affairs.

DISILLUSIONMENT AND INSTABILITY, 1920-1924

The Kapp *Putsch,* **1920.** The next danger signal for the Republic came from the Right. The old ruling class of militaristocrats and industrial leaders, driven into the background by the revolution, made a first bid to restore its power in March 1920. The leader of a plot to overthrow the government was Dr. Wolfgang Kapp, a banker of Königsberg and a founder of the Fatherland party. During the war Kapp had gained notoriety by venomous attacks on the policies of Chancellor Beth-mann-Hollweg. Among his co-conspirators in the contemplated *putsch* were General Walther von Lüttwitz, the aged commander of the First Army District in Berlin; Major Waldemar Pabst, a discharged officer, who took revenge on his government by organizing national-ist agitation; and Colonel Max Bauer, one of General Ludendorff's agents in intrigue. The old war lord Ludendorff was sympathetic with the aims of the conspiracy, but he decided to remain in the background.

In March 1920, according to the terms laid down by the Allies, the German government was obliged to dismiss between 50,000 and 60,000 men from the armed forces. Among the units slated for dissolution was a naval brigade commanded by Captain Hermann Ehrhardt, a notorious leader of the *Freikorps.* The brigade, reputed to be an effective fighting organization, had taken an important part in suppressing the soviet republic in Bavaria. Lüttwitz assured Ehrhardt that he would not allow the brigade to be disbanded.

On the evening of March 12, 1920, the Ehrhardt brigade went into action against the government. More than 5000 of its members marched a dozen miles from its military barracks to Berlin. Gustave Noske, minister of defense, had only about 2000 men to oppose the rebels. When he summoned his top military leaders, he learned to his dismay that they would not support the government. The generals had always been ready to put down Left-wing insurrections, but they were not willing to defend the Republic against its reactionary enemies. General Hans von Seeckt made it plain: "*Reichswehr* does not fire on *Reichswehr!*"

That same evening the government leaders, unable to defend Berlin, left by automobile for Dresden. Before leaving, they issued a call in the name of the Social Democratic party, for a general strike:

> Workers, comrades! The military *putsch* is under way. . . .
> We refuse to bow to this military pressure. We did not make the revolution in order to acknowledge once again the bloody rule of mercenaries. We will make no deal with the Baltic criminals. Workers, comrades! . . . Use every means to prevent the return of bloody reaction. Strike, stop working, strangle this military dictatorship, fight! . . . Not a hand must move, not a single worker must help the military dictatorship. General strike all along the line! Workers, unite!

Early the next morning the Ehrhardt brigade, unopposed, made a triumphant entry through the Brandenburg Gate. General Ludendorff was waiting for them. The men occupied government buildings and hoisted the old imperial colors. Kapp announced that he was chancellor. (*See Reading No. 19.*) The military leaders in eastern Germany declared themselves for the Kapp government, while those in western and southern Germany proclaimed their loyalty to the Republic.

From its beginning the Kapp *putsch* was an exercise in adult delinquency. Its leaders were weak and indecisive. There was no plan. The plotters were certain that the people of Berlin would greet them jubilantly, but they were soon disillusioned. Instead, there was solid resistance. The call for a general strike worked. There followed

one of the most effective stoppages the world had ever
seen up to that time. Without water, gas, electricity, and
transportation, Berlin was paralyzed. The coup degenerated into comic opera. Kapp requested the *Reichsbank*
to give him ten million marks to stabilize his regime, but
the bank officers declared they would honor the request
only if it were signed by an authorized official. There
was no such signature to be found.

Five days later, on March 17, 1920, Kapp, finding his
position untenable, announced his resignation and fled to
Sweden. His fellow conspirators sought refuge abroad.
The Ehrhardt brigade, deserted by its leaders, withdrew
from Berlin through jeering crowds. Kapp, ailing and
broken in spirit, returned to Germany and surrendered
to the authorities. He died in prison on June 12, 1922
while awaiting trial.

The Kapp *putsch,* a ludicrous fiasco, left a bad after-
taste. Several hundred people had lost their lives. More
seeds of political hatred and mistrust were sown. The
immediate danger of the Republic's overthrow from
the Right was over, but there was an uncomfortable feeling that the country was in serious trouble. Although
the revolt had been overcome by a general strike of the
workers, it was the officer corps which came out of the
rebellion with increased power. The *Reichswehr* was on
its way to becoming a state within the state.

Assassination of Erzberger, 1921. German politics
became increasingly brutalized. Matthias Erzberger
(1875-1921), a member of the Left wing of the Catholic
Center party, had entered the *Reichstag* in 1903. A gifted
and brilliant statesman, Erzberger took a leading role in
political affairs. During the war, on July 19, 1917, he
introduced a resolution in the *Reichstag* calling for peace
without annexations. On November 11, 1918, heading
the German delegation, he signed the armistice terms at
Compiègne. As minister of finance in the Bauer government (June 21, 1919-March 27, 1920) he signed the
Treaty of Versailles. For this action as a patriot he was
ridiculed by his countrymen. He was despised by nationalist conspirators, who made him their first victim.

On August 26, 1921, two former officers of the
Ehrhardt brigade, Schultz and Tillesen, who had taken

part in the Kapp *putsch,* lay in wait for Erzberger along a path in the Black Forest. They shot him down. The murderers, holding false passports, fled to Hungary, which refused to extradite them to Germany. German nationalists hailed the assassination as a just deed, as vengeance for Erzberger's journey to Compiègne. They conveniently disregarded the fact that Field Marshal von Hindenburg had been spared the humiliation of signing the armistice by Erzberger's willingness to take his place.

The Bombshell of Rapallo, 1922. Better relations with the new Soviet state became a cornerstone of the Republic's foreign policy. First among the motivating factors was the hatred shared by the Germans and Russians for the Allies. This was a response to the Allied claims that the Germans were seeking world domination on the battlefield and that the Russians were promoting world revolution. Secondly, leading German diplomats and army leaders were convinced that Bismarck's recommendation of close relations with Russia was logical and correct. General Hans von Seeckt, commander of the *Reichswehr,* held that it was to Germany's advantage to work with Russia in evading the constrictive military clauses of the Treaty of Versailles. Economically, highly industrialized Germany and agrarian Russia were said to be a "natural combination." Although they had no special love for Soviet Russia, policy-making German political leaders worked for a Russo-German *rapprochement.*

An opportunity came in April 1922, when the powers met at Genoa to discuss the problem of international financial obligations and especially the debts of the old Tsarist regime which the Communists had refused to acknowledge. For the first time after the war, Germans and Russians were invited to participate in a general European conference. They were pointedly ignored by the Allied representatives. Meanwhile, German and Russian agents were busily conducting negotiations to join together to create a counterweight to the overwhelming strength of the victor powers. The Genoa conference, crippled by French intransigence, accomplished nothing. On April 16, 1922, the German delegation, headed by Walther Rathenau, the foreign minister, and the Russian

group, led by Georgi Tschitscherin, slipped quietly away
from Genoa and went to the beautiful, nearby Riviera
resort of Rapallo. Here they signed a treaty which provided for resumption of diplomatic relations. Germany
relinquished claims for nationalized property of Germans in Russia, while the Russians, as a *quid pro quo*,
abandoned their demands for reparations from Germany.
The two countries agreed to extend to each other the
status of "most-favored nation" in their commercial relations. There was little that was astonishing about this
pact, which was immediately published. (*See Reading
No. 21.*)

The Allied powers, however, were appalled by a treaty
negotiated and signed under their very noses. They considered it to be a nightmare for Allied diplomacy and
denounced it as an invitation to disaster. The combined
military, economic, and political power of Russia and
Germany was regarded as a source of danger to the
West. Did it mean clandestine rearmament, or rebuilding
of the Red army, or another German drive for world
power? Angered, the Allied leaders began to take an
increasingly tough line toward Germany.

The Treaty of Rapallo was hailed inside Germany as
marking the end of the nation's postwar isolation and the
beginning of an independent foreign policy. Most German political parties, from Right to Left—monarchists,
democrats, and socialists alike—greeted it as a great
diplomatic coup. There were some reservations: some
Social Democrats feared that Russia would now flood
the country with Bolshevik propaganda, others were un-
easy about Germany's efforts to win the good will of the
rest of the world. Newspapers praised the treaty as "a
decision of world historical importance," as a "yes" to
Russia and as a "no" to the West. A similar reception
was accorded the pact in Russia. Leon Trotsky, in his
May Day, 1922, address, proclaimed that the great Red
army, "supported by our treaty with Germany," would
hurl back all enemies of the Soviet Union.

The political agreement reached at Rapallo was followed by a series of secret meetings between German
and Russian officers on problems of mutual military interest. Officers were transferred from one country to

the other for training. German scientists were invited to the Soviet Union to work on weapons forbidden by the Treaty of Versailles. Not until World War II was the extent of this collaboration revealed.

Murder of Rathenau, 1922.   The German architect of the Treaty of Rapallo was destined to survive it by little more than two months. Walther Rathenau (1867-1922), industrialist and statesman, was the son of Emil Rathenau, founder of the General Electric Society. The able heir assumed the responsibilities that wealth imposed upon him. At the outbreak of World War I, he foresaw the threat of the British blockade, and within a short time established a huge organization called the *Kriegsrohstoffabteilung* (KRA) (Division of Raw Materials for War). Using a threefold program of (1) regulation, (2) synthetic manufacture, and (3) substitute products (*Ersatzmittel*), Rathenau made it possible for Germany to continue the war for four years.

During the first year and a half of the Weimar Republic, German nationalists systematically sabotaged Allied policies and requirements. The new coalition government which came to power on May 10, 1921, under the Centrist leader, Dr. Joseph Wirth, initiated a policy of fulfillment. Rathenau, at first, minister of reconstruction and then foreign minister in the Wirth cabinet, believed that Germany was honor bound to carry out all pledges made by her peace delegates. "We Germans," he said, "are obligated by our signature, by the honor of our name. We recognize the binding character of our signatures, even though they do not express our wishes." Rathenau also negotiated the Rapallo pact with the Russians.

Nationalist hotheads were infuriated by Rathenau's policies. The fact that he was Jewish inflamed the hatred (*see Reading No. 22*):

> *Knallt ab den Juden Rathenau,*
> *Die gottverdammte Judensau!*

> (Shoot down Jew Rathenau,
>   The Goddamned swine of a Jewish sow.)

On June 23, 1922, Karl Helfferich, a German Nationalist leader, delivered a violent attack on Rathenau in the

Reichstag. Rathenau, he said, had pursued a policy of fulfillment which had brought about the devaluation of German money and the "pulverization of our middle class." The next morning, as Rathenau rode to the Foreign Office in an open automobile, he was followed by a large touring car, in which three young Nationalists, wearing long leather coats were seated. In the *Königsallee* one of the young men fired a submachine gun at Rathenau and the other hurled a grenade that almost tore him to shreds. Rathenau was left a shattered, bleeding corpse. (*See Reading No. 23.*)

In this barbaric fashion one of Germany's most able and respected statesmen was murdered. A patriot of great talent was rewarded with assassination. Rathenau's mother wrote to the mother of one of the plotters, both of whom belonged to "good" families: "In unspeakable sorrow I extend my hand to you, most suffering of women. . . . Had [your son] known my son, the noblest man the earth has ever borne, he would rather have killed himself than shot the other."

The assassination of Rathenau produced an emotional explosion among the republican elements inside Germany. There were great mass demonstrations at which demands were made that there be an end to political murder. The *Reichstag* passed a law for the protection of the Republic. Unregenerated Nationalists presented "extenuating circumstances"—the youthful assassins were motivated by "noble, patriotic motives" and should not be judged too harshly. Of the gunmen, Erwin Kern, a naval lieutenant, was slain by his pursuers; Hermann Fischer, an engineer, committed suicide; and Ernst Werner Techow, whose industrialist uncle was a friend of the Rathenau family, was sentenced to fifteen years in prison.

The Fall of the Wirth Cabinet. The death of Rathenau caused greater excitement than had Erzberger's assassination. For Wirth, chancellor since May 1921, it was a tragic loss. A former professor of natural science, Wirth had become the leader of the republican wing of the Catholic Center party. A democrat and a brilliant orator, Wirth had worked hand-in-hand with Rathenau to carry out Germany's treaty obligations

(*Erfüllungspolitik*). Both were anxious to take the reparations problem out of the arena of political friction and bring it into the realm of economics. Germany, they agreed, was morally committed to pay compensation for the damage done to the industrial areas of Belgium and northeastern France. "We Germans are obligated by our signature." This did not mean that Germans would halt their efforts to convince the Allies that reparations demands were well beyond what they could afford to pay.

The *Reichstag* approved the Wirth-Rathenau policy of fulfillment and accepted the Allied ultimatum on reparations payments. Nationalist opposition soared as a result of this "degradation." Attacks were made on "the Catholic Wirth and the Jew Rathenau." Rathenau's life was sacrificed to this violent opposition, and Wirth's political career did not survive this outburst of nationalistic frenzy. Wirth lost the support of the Social Democrats when he supported General von Seeckt's military machinations with the Russians. He resigned his office as chancellor on November 22, 1922. He was succeeded by Wilhelm Cuno, an independent in politics, who soon became embroiled in the reparations question.

Occupation of the Ruhr, 1923. The French, obsessed by a need for security, believed that it was to their advantage to control more of Germany's industry. In late 1922, without the cooperation or assent of the British, they decided to occupy the rich Ruhr area at the first favorable moment. The opportunity came on December 26, 1922, when a majority of the Allied Reparations Commission declared Germany to be in default on her deliveries of telegraph poles. (*See Reading No. 24.*) Backed by Belgium and with token support from Italy, the French, on January 11, 1923, sent troops into the Ruhr to enforce the terms of the Versailles treaty. The reason given for the occupation was "to protect French technicians who were running German mines and plants."

The problem was not only telephone poles but the entire matter of Franco-German relations. The French were convinced that the Germans had no intention of honestly abiding by the treaty and would surely cheat them. The Germans, on the other hand, suspected that

the French wanted to ruin their economy. It was the
old story of a thousand-year hatred: "We French and
Germans are like cats and dogs; we shall always fight one
another!"

The Germans reacted furiously to the Ruhr occupation. They were resentful and angry as leaders of
all political parties united to denounce French aggression.
Unable to reply with force, Germans in the Ruhr adopted
a policy of passive resistance. Workers went on a general strike and refused to enter mines or factories. The
sympathetic government in Berlin sent emissaries to the
Ruhr to organize and direct the resistance movement.
Workers sabotaged machinery and even attacked French
troops.

It soon became obvious that the French had acted
hastily and were in serious trouble. By now, however,
they had gone too far to retreat. British and American
public opinion condemned the occupation from the beginning, an attitude which made the French even more
determined to have their way. Believing that a show of
strength was necessary, they sent in even more troops.
They brought French workers into the Ruhr to operate
idle machines. The result was chaos. Accidents increased.
French engineers, unfamiliar with German locomotives,
ran them straight through their stations into the towns.
To German passive resistance the French responded by
forbidding the German police to wear uniforms and
bear arms, by dismissing customs officers, and by punish-
ing anyone guilty of interfering with the operation of the
railroads.

Meanwhile, the French supported the activities of
Rhineland separatists, who wanted to establish a new
Rhineland republic under French auspices. On March
31, 1923, in a clash between French troops and German
workers in the Krupp factories in Essen, thirteen persons were killed and thirty were wounded.

All Germany was thrown into excitement by the case
of Albert Leo Schlageter, a former *Freikorps* leader.
Arrested by the French criminal police in an Essen
hotel, he was accused of espionage and sabotage. A
French court in Düsseldorf sentenced him to death and

he was executed on May 26, 1923. (*See Reading No. 25.*) It is most probable that Schlageter was guilty of the charges against him. Had the case been reversed, a German military court would probably have found the same judgment against a Frenchman. To Germans, however, Schlageter was a martyr who had given his life for Germany. They denounced the execution as an inexcusable act of vengeance. Even the Communists, who did all they could in the Ruhr to make matters more chaotic, called Schlageter "a good soldier of the counter-revolution who deserves to be honored." Later, during the Hitler era, Schlageter was coupled with Horst Wessel in the Nazi pantheon of heroes. The character of both these "saints" left something to be desired, but they fitted perfectly into the Nazi pattern.

The French occupation of the Ruhr turned out to be a grotesque failure. It provoked a violent propaganda battle which neither side won. Franco-German hatred reached its highest level since the war years. The wounds caused by the occupation festered on both sides for many years. It dangerously undermined the already weak foundations of the Weimar Republic. Even the French economy was hurt by this attempt to beat Germany into submission long after the war had ended.

Runaway Inflation. French occupation of the Ruhr triggered an economic breakdown which led eventually to the collapse of the German mark. Before the war the mark was valued at 4.2 per dollar. During the war the mark began to drop slowly. The longer the British blockade continued, the greater became the volume of currency. This was not considered dangerous, for a certain amount of inflation took place during any protracted conflict. In 1919 the mark stood at 8.9 per dollar. Germany ended the war with a national debt of 144 billion marks, of which 89 billion were in long-term bonds and 55 billion in paper.

The inflationary situation was worsened by the great cost of demobilization and the confused events of the revolution. The presses began to print paper money faster and faster. At first, industrialists and merchants, even the general public, were not aware of the creeping inflation. The flood of new money swept shelves free of merchandise. The stock market became increasingly active.

By the middle of 1923 the value of the mark began to assume astronomical proportions. In November 1923 the mark sank to the value of 42 hundred million to the dollar. Prices began to rise tenfold, a hundred times, in a single day. A hundred-mark bill one day became a million-mark paper note the next day. The American dollar became the measure of value, and prices were adjusted to it rather than to the mark. Soon the printing presses could not keep up with the changing need for paper money. City governments began to issue their own emergency money printed on silk, linen, and even leather (*Notgeld*). Private concerns were given permission to overprint paper money. More than three hundred paper mills and two thousand printing shops worked around the clock to supply bank notes.

Germany was in a veritable fever dance. (*See Reading No. 26.*) There were extraordinary scenes. A woman who came to her butcher shop with a basketful of marks left them on the pavement as she followed the queue inside to get her meat. On her return she found her marks dumped into the gutter and the basket stolen. On streetcar rides the conductor did not accept fares until the end of the ride because the value of the mark would change in a matter of minutes. One could buy a night club or obtain the Emperor's box at the opera with a few dollar bills. Housewives had to shop several times a day, because a pound of butter might rise five times in cost within 24 hours. A week's subscription to a newspaper might cost a billion marks. Workers had to exchange six-weeks' pay (carted in wheelbarrows) for a pair of shoes. At one time it cost a billion marks to send a letter abroad.

There was a wild scramble for real goods of any kind. Barter replaced the money economy in many parts of the country. Huge fortunes were acquired within a few months by those who had access to foreign currencies. The effect was catastrophic for those with fixed incomes —with bank accounts, insurance policies, and pensions. The people who were wiped out lost all sense of security.

The productive middle class, traditionally the backbone of the country, was deprived of its property. Widows, civil servants, teachers, army officers, and pensioners lost their lifetime savings. Such unfortunates held tenaciously to their white-collar status to avoid being thrust down into the ranks of the despised proletariat. It was the scar that never healed. These were the people who later turned to Adolf Hitler as the messiah to lead them out of financial chaos.

It is incorrect and unjust to charge the German government with complicity in bringing about the inflation deliberately in order to pay reparations. The process of inflation was already under way when the French occupied the Ruhr. The French action merely accelerated the avalanche. The German government did contribute unwittingly by its reluctance to raise taxes at a time when reconstruction and welfare schemes were financed through deficit spending. Municipal improvements were financed through the issue of paper money rather than an increase in taxes. This helped unbalance the economy. The abolition of the gold standard, on August 4, 1914, also contributed to the inflationary process.

The entire problem was closely connected with the reparations demanded by the Allies from Germany for damage caused during the war. The Allies wanted no paper money: they were interested only in German productive capacity. Both Allied and German leaders learned the hard way, after the damage had been done, that the transfer of huge amounts of money in a highly unstable economy leads to critical economic dislocation.

Advent of Stresemann. In restoring public tranquillity, the Cuno government showed itself to be more concerned about proletarian radicals than about reactionaries on the Right. Its doom was sealed when the Social Democrats withdrew their support. On August 12, 1923, Cuno handed in his resignation as chancellor. He was succeeded by Gustav Stresemann (1878-1929). The son of a wholesale beer merchant, Stresemann had entered the *Reichstag* at the age of 28, where his remarkable oratorical talents attracted attention. During the war he had been a fervent monarchist and Pan-Germanist. In the era of the Weimar Republic he worked on the problems of reconstruction. Before he assumed the chancellorship he turned his attention to foreign affairs. He proposed a realistic attitude of collaborating with the victorious powers as long as might be necessary. This was the best way, he said, to obtain new concessions and to reduce the burdens imposed by the Treaty of Versailles. It was wrong, he intimated, to continue Cuno's policy of passive resistance, because it brought Germany nothing. Germany must try the path of conciliation.

After the occupation of the Ruhr, Stresemann made it clear to his countrymen that Germany must obtain a solution to the provoking problem of reparations. There must be cooperation between German and French industrialists. Germany must win the good will and trust of the victorious powers. He warned the Allies not to push the Germans too far, for in the background, he hinted, was the specter of Bolshevism.

The Beginnings of National Socialism. The future dictator of Germany, Adolf Hitler, was born on April 20, 1889, in the small village of Braunau on the River Inn between Austria and Germany. Both sides of his family came from a country district called the *Waldviertel,* or Woodlands, of Lower Austria. His father, Alois Schicklgrüber, the illegitimate son of a peasant woman, was a lonely, miserable border policeman, a veteran of three unhappy marriages. There was a continuous battle between father and son. In October 1907, after an indifferent education, Hitler, at the age of eighteen, came to Vienna. Supported by money sent by his mother, he had hopes of becoming a great artist. Then came the terrible blow of being refused entrance into the Vienna Academy of Fine Arts as a student. Hitler never recovered from this blow to his pride.

The next five years were the most miserable of his life. "I lived five years of woe in Vienna. I earned my living first as an apprentice and then as an unknown painter. Hunger was my faithful companion. My life was a continuous struggle with this pitiless friend." He lived in a home for derelicts and daily made the rounds of cafés and picture framers, trying to sell his drawings so that he could eat.

The start of World War I changed Hitler's life. "The

war came as a deliverance from the distress that had weighed upon me during the days of my youth. Over-powered by stormy enthusiasm, I fell upon my knees and thanked heaven from an overflowing heart." At the front Hitler proved himself to be an able soldier. He was crushed by news of the armistice. "What followed were terrible days and even worse nights. I knew that every-thing was lost. Only fools—or liars and criminals— could hope for mercy from the enemy. In these nights my hate grew against the men who had brought about this crime. I, however, decided to go into politics."

In the summer of 1919 Hitler became member number seven of a small group of restless men who called them-selves the German Worker's party. The party had no program, no plan of action. It was merely "against" the government. It had only 7.5 marks (less than $2.00) in its treasury. The group held its meetings in the back room of a Munich café. Here Hitler discovered his talent as an orator. "I could speak! After 30 minutes the people in the tiny room were electrified." Intoxicated by his own voice, Hitler denounced the Treaty of Versailles in gutter terms. "I spoke until I had before me a surging mass of sacred, boundless wrath."

On February 24, 1920, a committee of the small party drafted a twenty-five point program. (*See Reading No. 20.*) It was designed to win the support of all discon-tented people: war veterans, students, monarchists, shop-keepers, workers, businessmen, anti-Semites, anti-Catho-lics, anti-liberals, anti-Socialists, anti-Communists. Every German with a grudge against the Republic was wel-comed. The authors of the program borrowed heavily from socialist ideology in order to attract mass support. At the same time, Point 16, one of the most important sections of the program, asked for "creation and mainte-nance of a healthy middle class." With its program set, the party now changed its name to the National Socialist German Workers' Party (NSDAP). The term Nazi came from the first two words of the German name—*NAtional SoZIalist*. Under its emotional, shrieking leader, the party began a drive for political power.

Hitler's Beer-Hall *Putsch*, 1923.   On the evening of November 8, 1923, about 3,000 Germans were gathered

in the *Bürgerbräu Keller,* one of the largest beer halls
in Munich, to hear a speech by Gustav von Kahr, State
Commissioner of Bavaria. Present were the most important governmental, military, and social leaders of
Bavaria, including General Otto von Lossow, commander
of the armed forces in Bavaria, and Colonel Hans von
Seisser, head of the Bavarian secret police. The crowd
was unaware that it would soon share a highly emotional
experience.

In the darkness the hall was surrounded by 600 Nazi
S.A. men (*Sturmabteilung*—storm troopers). A machine
gun was set up outside with its mouth pointed to the
front door. Someone slammed the door shut from the
inside. While Kahr was droning on in his speech, down
the aisle came a wildly excited little man with a Charlie
Chaplin mustache. He was surrounded by a group of
tough henchmen.

Hitler jumped on a chair, fired a shot at the ceiling,
and in the sudden silence, screamed: "The national
revolution has broken out! The hall is filled with 600
armed men. Nobody is allowed to leave. The Bavarian
government and the government at Berlin are deposed.
A new government will be formed at once. The barracks
of the *Reichswehr* and the police barracks are occupied.
Both have rallied to the swastika!" The last sentences
were lies: neither army nor police knew anything about
the attempted *putsch.*

Hitler ordered Kahr, Lossow, and Seisser to follow
him to a small side room. He lectured them in great
agitation, saying that he was forming a new government
with the war hero, General Ludendorff. The three men,
although nervous, began to recover their courage. They
berated Hitler and asked what he meant by this con-
founded nonsense. The Nazi leader flew into a rage. He
dashed back into the hall and shouted to the crowd:
"Tomorrow will find a national government in Germany, or it will find us dead!"

At this critical moment Ludendorff arrived. He denounced Hitler for starting a revolution without letting
him know in advance. Hitler ignored the slight. Beaming
with joy, he told the crowd that victory was his and that

he had at last fulfilled "the oath I swore five years ago as a blind cripple in a military hospital."

All through the night a struggle for power went on in the beer hall. One by one, Kahr, Lossow, and Seisser managed to escape. When the news was flashed to Berlin, General von Seeckt, commander of the *Reichswehr,* sent word that he would smash the rebellion if Munich could not do it.

By the next morning Hitler realized that he had failed. There was too much military and police power against him. He wanted to call the whole thing off. But Ludendorff, with fighting instincts aroused, insisted that there be no retreat.

At eleven in the morning on November 9, 1923, Nazi storm troopers, bearing swastika flags and war banners, marched toward the Marienplatz in the center of Munich. They pushed aside the small police squads which tried to stop them. At the head of the demonstrators were Hitler, Ludendorff, Hermann Goering, aviator hero of the war, and Julius Streicher, an anti-Semitic agitator. As the parade came to the Odeonplatz near the *Feldherrnhalle,* a hall constructed to honor German military heroes, the way was barred by a detachment of police holding carbines. In this confrontation there were a hundred police and 3,000 Nazis.

Hitler cried: "Surrender! Surrender!" The answer was a hail of lead. Within a minute, sixteen Nazis and three policemen lay dead on the pavement. Many others were wounded and groaning. Goering, shot through the thigh, fell to the ground. Hitler, an alert-dispatch bearer during the war, automatically hit the pavement as soon as he heard the crack of guns. He managed to escape. Ludendorff, like an aged, fearless Siegfried, his eyes staring ahead, marched straight through the ranks of the police, who respectfully turned their guns aside. (*See Reading No. 27.*)

The *putsch* failed. Hitler was arrested and tried for treason. At the trial he delivered a harangue (*see Reading No. 28*) as if he were at a mass meeting of the world. He was found guilty and sentenced to five years in Landsberg prison. Here, as a kind of celebrated guest, he served

eighteen and a half months. With the assistance of
Rudolf Hess, his beetle-browed secretary and confidant,
he wrote *Mein Kampf* (*My Battle*), which became the
bible of the Nazi movement. (*See Reading No. 29.*)

Hitler's attempted *coup d'état,* despite its failure, was a
remarkable achievement for a political nobody. In only
a few hours, by sheer gall and bluff, he had transformed
his unimportant movement into a major opponent of the
government. He had turned his trial for treason into a
personal triumph. There was great political talent here.
Hitler learned an important lesson at the beer hall—his
movement was not strong enough to win power by direct
action. Instead, he saw that it was necessary to arouse the
enthusiasm of the masses plus the support of moneyed
and influential people. He would conquer the Weimar
Republic and achieve power by legal means.

Rearmament: Role of the *Reichswehr*.   The fourth
of Wilson's Fourteen Points reads as follows:

> 4. Adequate guarantees given and taken that national
> armaments will be reduced to the lowest point consistent
> with domestic safety.

Moreover, Wilson had proposed world-wide disarmament.
And the first paragraph of Article 8 of the Covenant of
the League of Nations read:

> The Members of the League recognize that the maintenance
> of peace requires the reduction of national armaments to
> the lowest point consistent with national safety and the en-
> forcement by common action of international obligations.

Germans who insisted that they had laid down their
arms on the basis of the Fourteen Points were angered
by the unilateral disarmament clauses of the Treaty of
Versailles. When the Great Powers retained or enlarged
their armaments, the Germans cried foul. Why were
Germans the only ones to be disarmed? Were not Germans the victims of a wicked plot to maintain their
weakness?

The German military never resigned itself to this state
of affairs. The *Reichswehr,* the national army, and such
semimilitary organizations as the *Stahlhelm* (steel hel-

met), the major veterans' group, were most dissatisfied. The Treaty of Versailles had stipulated the size, organization, term of service, armament, and rate of personnel turnover allowed the German military. This was the victors' decision. To German military men it was an unwarranted and unjust interference in the internal affairs of their country.

The Republic, in the first years of its existence, desperately needed a military organization to take the place of the old Imperial army. The men of Weimar, instead of building a new democratic army, turned to the old leaders of the army for assistance. The rebirth of the German army was the result of this alliance. The common objective of the Majority Socialists and the old soldiers was the restoration of order. Separately, they would have been helpless to stem the growing chaos. Together, despite their divergent ideological aims, they might save the Republic. The military-civilian partnership nearly foundered during the Kapp *putsch* in March 1920, the first revolt of the disinherited to plague the Republic. But it weathered that storm. The great problem for the government was an old one in German history —how to keep the militaristocrats under civilian control. The relationship was always a precarious one. (*See Reading No. 30.*)

The reconstruction of the German army was primarily the work of General Hans von Seeckt (1866-1936). Born in Schleswig, the son of a general, he joined his father's regiment, First Grenadier Guards, and transferred to the General Staff in 1899. During the war he fought as a lieutenant-colonel under von Kluck in Flanders (1914), and under Mackensen (1915). In December 1917 he served with the Turkish army, and remained in the East until the armistice. A hard-working and able officer, he was given command of the *Reichswehr* in 1920 and served as its head for six years.

Seeckt was responsible for the secret rearmament of Germany under the very noses of the Allied Disarmament Commission in Berlin. He had two goals: (1) to build up the *Reichswehr* under difficult conditions; and (2) to support German-Russian military cooperation directed against the West.

The first task called for ingenuity and shrewdness. Limited by the peace treaty to an army of a hundred thousand men and no conscription, Seeckt made certain that each man in the army had the ability and the potential of a highly trained officer. His army was small in size, but efficient and superior in training and equipment. It had great mobility and its leaders were imbued with a fluid concept of strategy. Seeckt saw to it that his men understood the spirit and traditions of the old Imperial army. He rejected most volunteers from the *Freikorps* on the ground that they understood nothing of discipline and were enmeshed in politics. He gave responsible posts to young men of the "better families," most of whom had little respect for the Weimar Republic. For manpower he depended upon the semimilitary organizations and the squads of the political parties. He successfully urged industrialists to tool their factories so that they would be ready for military production. He encouraged civil aviation and glider clubs to train young men.

Seeckt's second task was to work closely with the Russians. He sent German officers to help Lenin reorganize the Red army. He encouraged German industrialists to organize war factories in Russia to produce planes and tanks, the key weapons denied Germany by the peace treaty. Both the Red army and the *Reichswehr* profited. The Russians received the benefit of professional advice from experts, while the Germans were able to get training privileges inside the Soviet Union. In Russian factories, far from the eyes of the Allied Disarmament Commission, German armaments experts experimented with planes, tanks, and heavy guns. The Allies were aware of this situation, but there was little they could do about it. Dissension among the Allies favored the secret armament of Germany. The British, unlike the French, were not opposed to the idea of a stronger Germany, especially because it suited London's concept of a balance of power on the Continent.

— 6 —

THE ERA OF OPTIMISM AND CONCILIATION, 1924-1929

The Dawes Plan, 1924. On October 16, 1923, several weeks before the Hitler-Ludendorff *putsch*, the government took several important steps to meet the monetary crisis. It set up the new *Rentenbank* to issue currency, and introduced a new currency, called the *Rentenmark* (based on landed values). At the same time it took steps to balance the budget. Responsibility for these major changes was placed on two men: Hans Luther, the minister of finance, and Hjalmar Horace Greeley Schacht, economist, financier, and member of the Democratic party. Schacht, as special currency commissioner, immediately stopped the printing of paper money, the extent of which had reached astronomical proportions. He gave the *Rentenmark* an equal value to the old gold *Reichsmark* of prewar days. The German people mortgaged their entire personal resources as coverage for the new mark. Some observers regarded this as a display of patriotism, others dismissed it as a colossal bluff. But the important thing was that it worked. Within a few weeks, Schacht received his reward by being appointed president of the *Reichsbank*, Germany's most influential financial institution.

In January 1924, the Reparation Commission appointed a committee consisting of two representatives each from the United States, Great Britain, France, Italy, and Belgium, under the chairmanship of Charles G. Dawes, an American financial expert. The new committee's task was to examine Germany's capacity to pay reparations and to make appropriate recommendations. Its report, submitted to the Reparation Commission on April 9, 1924, came to be known as the Dawes Plan. (*See Reading No. 31.*)

The Dawes report made the following recommendations: (1) The Ruhr was to be evacuated. (2) A central bank of issue, consisting of seven Germans and seven foreigners, was to be a repository for reparation payments. (3) Reparation payments would commence at 240 million dollars the first year and gradually rise over a period of four years to a standard annuity of 600 million dollars. (4) The standard annuity might be raised or lowered in line with an index of prosperity based on the period 1927-1929. (5) Deliveries in kind during the first year were to be financed by an international loan of 200 million dollars. (6) The money for reparation payments was to be obtained from a transport tax, railway bonds, industrial debentures, and revenues from beer, tobacco, sugar, and customs. (7) A foreign Agent General of Reparation Payments would be stationed inside Germany (S. Parker Gilbert, an American financier, was appointed to this position).

The German government had many reservations in mind, but nevertheless, on April 15, 1924, it gave the Reparation Commission an affirmative answer. There were, indeed, weaknesses in the plan. It was still a stopgap solution. It irritated the Germans because it called for foreign control over their finances. It made the annual total of reparations due from Germany dependent upon an index of prosperity: the more prosperous the Germans became the more they had to pay. Most discouraging of all, it set no final total of indebtedness. Apparently, the Germans would continue to make large payments without knowing how long they were required to keep up the payments.

While it helped with the immediate problem, the Dawes Plan actually promoted a cycle harmful for international finance. American funds poured into Germany; Germany used the money to pay reparations; Britain and France, which received most of this money, were supposed to pay their war debts to the United States; the United States sent more money to Germany. The German fell into the habit of expecting that funds from the United States would flow on indefinitely. That assumption would be challenged shortly when American investors retreated from the international market.

Political Repercussions. In the difficult situation following the Hitler-Ludendorff *putsch*, Stresemann resigned the chancellorship (November 30 1923). A week later Wilhelm Marx, Centrist leader, became chancellor, with Stresemann remaining in charge of the foreign office. The Marx government contained no representative of labor and, in general, favored a conservative course. It called for restoration of law and order, stabilization of the currency, and revived economic life.

On March 13, 1924, President Ebert dissolved the *Reichstag* and called for new elections. The primary issue at hand was the Dawes report. The Nationalists undertook a countrywide campaign to discredit the recommendations of the experts. Germans, they said, must reject a scheme which made them sacrifice financial sovereignty and place their banking institutions under foreign control. Stresemann answered these charges by pointing out that Germany had to be rid of her financial chains and had to win the good will of the rest of the world.

The elections of May 1924 resulted in a victory for the opponents of the Dawes report. The Nationalists polled a popular vote of 5,718,543, some two million more than they had received in June 1920. The number of Nationalist seats in the *Reichstag* rose from sixty-six to ninety-six. Both Nazis and Communists showed increased strength in the new *Reichstag*. The Social Democrats, the People's party, and the Democrats all lost ground. Despite opposition, the Dawes report was approved by the *Reichstag* by a vote of 247 to 183.

Prosperity and Boom Days. The country was still beset by political troubles, but economically the picture was changed. Bolstered by the Dawes plan, the economy made a surprising recovery. The distressing days of the inflation were forgotten as the people tasted prosperity. It was a spectacular development, to be compared with the equally rapid economic revival of Germany after the nightmare of Hitler's war. True, the coating was thin, and the wounds underneath had never completely healed, but for the time being, at least, happy days were back again.

Behind the fast rate of recovery were two factors, one external and one internal (both were to be repeated after World War II). First, foreign capital, chiefly from the United States, flowed into Germany in the form of both short-term and long-term loans. German securities, sold abroad, brought capital into the country. From 1924 to 1929 more than 8 billion dollars in foreign loans, mostly in short-term commitments, flowed into Germany at a time when she was paying less than 2 billion dollars in reparations. This considerable profit was used not only to revive industry but also to support public works, extend social services, and pay for subsidies to agriculture.

The economy bloomed under this help from abroad. Cities built huge complexes of stadiums (the Frankfort *Stadion* included swimming pools for youngsters and adults, racing fields for bicycles and motorcycles, and other similar arenas). Great clusters of apartment houses and lavish new opera houses were built. With new money in circulation, wages rose. Although there were still problems to be solved, people in general breathed easier in an atmosphere of affluence.

The second factor in this seeming economic success of the Republic was internal. German industry and labor worked together and concentrated their energies on recovery. Factory owners started with new machinery, unlike their British counterparts who retained the old machines because they still had life in them. German industrialists were stimulated by American methods of scientific management. They mastered the lessons of mass production, including standardization of patterns, interchangeable parts, improved methods of accounting, and advertising designed to promote sales and distribution. The government helped by encouraging scientific research in the institutions of higher learning.

The cartel system, which Germany had developed for many decades, was further extended. The great enterprises were used to protect invested capital, eliminate competition, stabilize profits, and avoid business cycles. They fixed prices, divided markets, and regulated foreign trade. They tended toward monopoly, but German industrialists were certain that cartels helped them escape from economic anarchy.

The German cartels—*Hapag* in shipping, *Siemens* in cement, and the *Vereinigte Stahlwerke* in steel—enjoyed a world-wide reputation. By far the greatest was the *Interessen Gemeinschaft der Farben Industrie,* commonly known as *I. G. Farben,* the world's most powerful industrial combination. This giant trust, consolidated in 1925, controlled nearly four hundred firms scattered over the country, along with some five hundred enterprises abroad, all in a closely interlocking relationship. It made thousands of agreements. It manufactured a large variety of products which it distributed throughout the world. It had at its command an army of scientists, industrialists, statesmen, even economic spies. A huge economic octopus, it used its restrictive power of patent tie-ups with foreign industrialists to slow up production of strategic war materials in countries which the Germans considered to be potential enemies.

Along with the concentration of industry went an increased organization of labor unions and greater legal recognition of their place in the national economic structure. The Weimar constitution had guaranteed every German the opportunity to earn his living by productive labor. The new trade unions, recognized as spokesmen for the workers, were encouraged to negotiate for collective contracts. By 1929, union membership totaled 5,470,000. The unions, with strong support from the courts, were able to bring about a rise in wages. Average real wages increased by 6 per cent from 1914 to 1929. The traditional system of social security, initiated by Bismarck, was strengthened and extended by the adoption of unemployment insurance.

This was the picture of the Weimar Republic in the middle 1920's—political troubles and economic well-being. There would be difficulties if the economy slowed down. The next economic crisis, the world depression of 1929, would hit Germany with tremendous impact.

The Death of Ebert.   The life of any politician in the Weimar Republic was filled with vicissitudes. Friedrich Ebert, president of the Republic, was no exception.

A plain man of the people, he was battered unmercifully from both Right and Left. Conservatives received with ill grace the spectacle of a former saddler holding the highest office in the land. Radicals cursed him because he had jailed their leaders and declined to become a catspaw for a soviet revolution. The Communists damned him especially, as a tool of the bourgeoisie. He had led his country through six years of bitter politics on the home front and great pressures from abroad. He had done his task well: he had rescued Germany from utter collapse after four years of war and months of civil strife. But there was little sense of gratitude.

Ebert was the victim of a slanderous attack accusing him of seditious conduct and of breaking the back of the army. A certain Herr Rothard, of undistinguished background, published a letter accusing Ebert of treasonable conduct in connection with the munitions workers' strike of 1918. It was a canard of the lowest order—Ebert had lost two sons in the war. The president was goaded into bringing an action for libel against Rothard. The court found Rothard technically guilty and sentenced him to three months' imprisonment. However, it went on to find that, according to the criminal code, Ebert had, in fact, committed treason in joining the strike. Nationalist orators and journalists pounced on this verdict as a gift from heaven and repeated it *ad nauseam*. Government officials and many citizens hastened to assure the president of their confidence and sympathy as he appealed the case.

During this time Ebert delayed a necessary operation to await the result of the legal action. He was tortured day and night by worry over the injustice done to him. According to Noske, he was "literally scourged to death by the shameful persecution which, during his final illness, he was forced to suffer at the hands of an egregious, vulgar press."

On February 25, 1925, after repeated attacks of appendicitis and accompanying peritonitis, Ebert died. He was only fifty-four. Here was another German statesman hounded to his death in an age of tawdry politics. Even after his death he was cursed by many who should have been grateful for his work.

Election of Hindenburg, 1925. For the first time

in their history the German people were charged with the task of electing a chief executive. The instability of public opinion in the past several years was an important factor at his critical moment. It was certain that the reactionary and conservative forces would make a strong bid to elect their own man and strike a blow at democracy in the new Germany. To avoid this calamity it was necessary that Social Democrats and Communists stand together against a turn to the Right. But the traditional feud between the two parties, instead of being eased, became more and more aggravated.

The election hinged on the figure of a celebrated war hero. Paul Ludwig Hans Anton von Beneckendorff und von Hindenburg (1847-1934), "the man with three lives," was the descendant of a long line of soldiers in Prussian service. In the Austro-Prussian War of 1866, his first campaign, he was wounded in the head. As a lieutenant in the Third Regiment of Foot Guards, he entered Paris with the victorious Prussian army in 1871. He served in the army for another four decades without any special distinction.

Hindenburg's second life began in 1914 at the age of 67. He was recalled to help stop the Russian advance in East Prussia. Together with General Ludendorff, he won decisive victories at Tannenberg and the Masurian Lakes. He was made a field marshal in December 1914. From July 1917 to the Armistice, Hindenburg, together with Ludendorff, acted as dictators of Germany. Hindenburg's image was inflated by propaganda to a point where he appeared to the people to be a legendary Titan. A huge wooden statue of him was erected in the *Königsplatz* in Berlin, and people paid varying sums to drive good-luck silver or iron nails into the effigy. *Der eiserne Hindenburg* ("the iron Hindenburg") sparkled in the midday sun. In November 1918 Hindenburg advised William II to leave Germany. The old general remained in charge of German troops until July 1919. He then retired to Neudeck.

Following the death of Ebert, Germans went to the polls on March 29, 1925 to elect a new president. Dr. Karl Jarres, mayor of Duisburg and minister of the interior under Stresemann and Marx, received 10.7 million votes; Otto Braun, the Social Democratic candidate, 7.8 million; Wilhelm Marx, center, 4 million; Ernst Thälmann, Communist *Reichstag* delegate, 1.8 million; Dr. Willy Hugo Hellpach, president of Baden and candidate of the Democratic party, 1.5 million; Heinrich Held, Bavarian People's party, almost 1 million; and General Ludendorff, 200,000. No candidate received a required majority on this ballot. A second election was in order, with only a plurality necessary to win.

For the runoff election the Nationalists proposed the name of Hindenburg as a national figure who stood above party divisions. Stresemann, leader of the People's party, did his best to discourage the old man from running. He knew that, to the Allies, Hindenburg symbolized that brutal lust for war which they had defeated after four years of strife. They would regard his candidacy as a slap at the Treaty of Versailles. But the matter soon snowballed out of Stresemann's control. Both Stresemann and the People's party decided to support the aged field marshal. The republican groups joined their forces to support Wilhelm Marx. The Communists had to make a crucial choice. Would they help strengthen the Republic by supporting the democratic parties? They renominated their own candidate, Thälmann, who would receive the same number of votes as in the first election, thereby making certain the election of Hindenburg.

On April 26, 1925, the Germans went to the polls. Hindenburg received 14.6 million votes (48 per cent of all those cast); Marx, 13.7 million; Thälmann, 1.9 million. Hindenburg had won by a margin of 904,151 votes. It was not an absolute majority, but the constitution did not require one. If only one half of the Communist vote had gone to Marx, Hindenburg would have been beaten. The entire course of German and world history might have been directed into different channels.

On May 11, 1925, Hindenburg arrived in Berlin and was received by the people with a tumultuous welcome. The flags displayed were the black-white-red banners of the Empire, not the black-red-gold of the Republic. The next day Hindenburg took his oath of office and began the third of his three lives. He issued a proclamation to the people promising to exercise justice for all, to serve the interests of the nation as a whole, and to work to free the nation from the "unjust stains on its character." (*See Reading No. 32.*)

The outcome of the election produced consternation among the Allies. It was felt that a man without the slightest bond to the new state had been elected, a man who had openly acknowledged his monarchist sympathies, and who would have been delighted to return the reins of power to the hands of another Hohenzollern. The historian Erich Eyck wrote: "No matter how Hindenburg might comport himself in the immediate future, his election as president of Germany was a triumph of nationalism and militarism and a heavy defeat for the Republic and parliamentary government."

The old man fooled his critics. Certainly he must have had only contempt for the regime which he was serving. It was different from every authoritarian fiber of his own being. But he had taken an oath, and to a Prussian field marshal that oath was a sacred thing. For the next five years, until early 1930, he showed the most careful respect for parliamentarian principles. He was faithful to the letter and the spirit of the Weimar constitution. The monarchists who had supported him were overcome with rage, but there was nothing they could do about it for the time being.

The Role of Stresemann.   Gustav Stresemann, who had been German chancellor for a few months in 1923, was thereafter foreign minister continuously until his death in 1929. So important was he in German history during that time that the period is often referred to as the Stresemann era. He held the threads of foreign policy in his hands. He worked diligently to relieve Germany from the burdens of Versailles. As a realist he was aware that it was plainly impossible for Germany to bludgeon her way out of her bonds. Germany was far too weak to seek improvement of her position by force. In the climate of his day, Stresemann preferred the carrot to the bayonet.

After Stresemann's death, a letter which he had sent to the former German crown prince on September 7, 1925, brought serious doubts about his sincerity in promoting a peace program. In this letter Stresemann described what he believed to be the main goals of German foreign policy. It was necessary, he said, to solve the reparations problem in a manner bearable for Germany, so that she might have the necessary peace and security that were prerequisite for her "renewal of strength." Germany's frontiers, he said, must be rectified, despite Versailles. There must be *Anschluss* (union) with Austria. "German policy will have to be, as Metternich said of Austria after 1809, '*zu finassieren*' (from the French, *finesser:* to act with subterfuge)." Stresemann's critics quoted this letter as a perfect example of his duplicity. His entire policy, they charged, had been devised to cover up for Germany as she recouped her armed strength. His aim was to lull France into a sense of security while he built German strength for a later showdown. This man, with his reputation for compromise, good will, and peace, they said, was really a monarchist at heart, a clever manipulator whose integrity and sincerity left something to be desired.

Sweetness and Light: Locarno, 1925.   Stresemann was the architect of Locarno and the subsequent era of international good will. A few days after the inauguration of President Hindenburg, Stresemann presented himself to report his plans for foreign policy. To find a *modus vivendi,* a mode of living with France and the Allies, was a cardinal aim of his diplomacy. He would seek an international agreement that would give France her desperately wanted sense of security against German aggression. Hindenburg, reared in a tradition of enmity to France, must have been astonished by the boldness of his foreign minister.

It was not altogether a new suggestion. Late in 1922, Chancellor Cuno had proposed a regional pact guaranteeing the western border of Germany and at the same time satisfying French demands for security. Stresemann reasoned that if the Germans recognized the loss of Alsace and Lorraine and guaranteed the *status quo* along the Rhine, the French would be appeased and would not be likely to oppose the Germans on the international scene.

Stresemann worked closely with Austen Chamberlain, the British prime minister, and with Aristide Briand, the

French premier. On February 9, 1925, he sent notes to London and Paris suggesting a regional pact guaranteeing the western frontier of Germany. London seemed friendly. But Paris replied that France would be interested if a similar guarantee were also given for Germany's eastern borders, touching France's allies Poland and Czechoslovakia. Stresemann refused to accept this stipulation. The French replied on June 16, 1925, accepting the proposed mutual security treaty in the west with the understanding that Germany was to join the League of Nations. Since this was an era of "open covenants openly arrived at," the German memorandum and the French reply were published simultaneously in the press of both countries and of the world. Negotiations continued for the next several months.

Meanwhile, inside Germany there was violent criticism of Stresemann and his plan. Chancellor Luther had taken German Nationalists into his first cabinet in January 1925, and now they began to cause trouble. They were appalled by the possibility of renouncing Alsace-Lorraine: to them this was not only a national disgrace but sheer lunacy. The military, too, was getting restless. General von Seeckt spoke bluntly: "We must acquire power, and as soon as we have power, we will naturally retake all that we have lost." This call for revenge was exactly the opposite of what Stresemann was trying to do. On the far Left, Communists reviled Stresemann for "offering German soil for a future war against Soviet Russia as the price of reconciliation with France and England." Stresemann, they charged, was a "betrayed betrayer."

Despite the criticism, Stresemann pushed ahead. In October 1925 a conference was called at Locarno, a peaceful city on the Swiss shore of Lake Maggiore. Attending were representatives from Great Britain, Germany, France, Italy, Belgium, Poland, and Czechoslovakia. The Big Three—Stresemann, Chamberlain, and Briand—worked together to remove obstacles that littered the road to agreement.

After the most difficult negotiations came the five Locarno treaties of 1925. The Treaty of Mutual Guarantee (*see Reading No. 33*) provided for the main-

tenance of the territorial *status quo* and the inviolability
of the borders between Germany, France, and Belgium.
Germany thereby recognized the permanence of her
western frontier as set by the Treaty of Versailles. The
contracting partners agreed that in no case would they
resort to war against each other to rectify the frontier. In
four additional arbitration treaties with France, Belgium,
Poland, and Czechoslovakia, Germany agreed that she
would not seek to revise her eastern borders by unilateral
action.

The Locarno Pact was signed on October 16, 1925. A
few days later the German Nationalist ministers resigned
from the cabinet. On November 23 the cabinet presented
the issue to the *Reichstag*. After some debate, the treaties
were ratified by a vote of 300 to 174. The *Reichstag* also
approved Germany's application to the League of Nations by a vote of 275 to 183.

All the world reacted favorably to the "spirit of Locarno." In the general euphoria it was believed that the
era of wars was now ended, to be succeeded by a time
of peace and international good will. A first step had
been taken in halting the thousand-year enmity between
Germany and France. For the first time since the war
Germans and Frenchmen had worked together in har-
mony. This would surely lead to further concord and
conciliation.

On the other hand there were skeptics inside Germany.
The German Nationalists roundly denounced the "sell-
out" of Locarno and accused Stresemann of traitorously
abandoning Alsace and Lorraine, "integral parts of the
Fatherland." Stresemann eloquently defended the pact in
speeches justifying his course. (*See Reading No. 34.*)

There was some criticism, too, in the Allied countries.
Perhaps Stresemann was trying to lull France into a
sense of security while driving a wedge into Anglo-
French relations. Some spoke of "appeasement." Others
pointed to the fact that the French began building their
Maginot Line, an indication that they had little faith in
German promises.

The League of Nations. German Communists ex-
coriated the League of Nations as "a consortium of ban-
dits for the purpose of sugar-coating war with idealism."

Nevertheless, the way had been prepared for Germany's entrance into the world organization. On February 1, 1926, the evacuation of the Cologne zone of occupation was completed by the Allies. Two days later, by a vote of eighteen to eight, the *Reichstag* Committee on Foreign Affairs approved Stresemann's suggestion that Germany formally request admission to the League. Stresemann argued successfully that, as a member of the League, the *Reich* would be in a better position to work for revision of the Treaty of Versailles.

A meeting of the Council and Assembly of the League was called on March 8, 1926, especially for the purpose of acting on the German application. There were unforeseen complications. It had been understood that Germany would have a permanent seat on the Council, which would have made her a peer among her former enemies (Great Britain, France, Italy, and Japan). For the Republic this recognition as a great power was important and essential. But Poland, Brazil, Spain, China, Czechoslovakia, and Persia introduced a discordant note by demanding that they, too, be made permanent members of the Council. The issue seemed headed for interminable debate. For the time being, Germany's entrance into the League was stalled.

Inside Germany there was an even greater debate in the *Reichstag* and among the German public. German Nationalists heatedly demanded that Germany retract her request for admission. They introduced a no-confidence motion in Chancellor Luther's second cabinet, which failed by a vote of 260 to 141.

The Russo-German Treaty, 1926. The matter of Germany's admission to the League of Nations was complicated by Russo-German relations. Alarmed by the Western orientation of German policy, especially the Locarno treaties, the Russians feared that the Germans were turning their backs on Rapallo. Moscow was disturbed by Article 16 of the League covenant by which Germany conceivably might be called to the defense of Poland. All this, the Russians were certain, was part of a shrewd plot to isolate the Soviet Union. The Russians called for another treaty with Germany. They argued that, since the Locarno powers could not even push through a simple matter such as Germany's entrance into the League, it was foolish for Germany to depend on the Western powers for more serious assistance.

Stresemann found himself in a dilemma. He knew that another pact with Russia would probably be greeted favorably inside Germany, but at the same time he had to be sure that it would not be taken as a blow at the Locarno treaties or as another obstacle to Germany's admission into the League. He was careful to notify the French and British governments before the pact was concluded.

The Russo-German treaty, signed on April 24, 1926 at Berlin, extended the Rapallo agreement of 1922. (*See Reading No. 35.*) There were only four articles. The first stated that Rapallo remained the basis of Russo-German relations. The second pledged either party to neutrality in the event that the other should be attacked by one or more powers. The third article stated that neither party would join any coalition for the purpose of an economic or financial boycott of the other. The fourth set the duration of the treaty at five years.

This pact, which converted Russo-German friendship into a virtual alliance, was received with jubilation inside Germany. All parties supported it in the *Reichstag*. The *Reichstag* Committee on Foreign Affairs, usually throttled by bitter arguments, gave it unanimous approval. On June 26, 1926, the *Reichstag* ratified the treaty, with only three dissenting votes.

The treaty created a great sensation abroad. With the exception of the British, who believed that the pact might result in closer contact between the League and Russia, most Europeans expressed renewed suspicion of Germany. The Russo-German agreement, some observers said, placed the Locarno treaties in jeopardy. The Poles, especially, were angered by the prospect of being caught in a Russo-German vise. Stresemann did what he could to allay suspicions, as indicated in this radio broadcast:

This treaty has nothing sensational in it. On the contrary, it is quite natural (*selbstverständlich*). An age-old friendship unites our two countries. From Frederick the Great down to the Great War they had never taken up arms against each other. Economically, they were bound together. Germany could not live without Russia's agricultural products, and Russia could not do without our industry.

Germany Enters the League.   Despite the international friction over the Treaty of Berlin, the "spirit of Locarno" prevailed. On September 8, 1926, by unanimous vote of the Assembly, Germany was admitted to the League of Nations. A compromise was arranged by which Germany was given a permanent seat on the Council and three more nonpermanent seats were allotted to Poland, Spain, and Brazil. The solution was accepted by all concerned, with the exception of Brazil, which resigned from the League.

With League membership Germany placed herself under the authority of a body strongly influenced by France. It also meant German recognition of the Treaty of Versailles, of which the covenant of the League was a part. Stresemann regarded this as an acceptable bargain, for it gave Germany a new forum for presenting her grievances to the world. His first speech to the League, however, was couched in friendly terms, with a gentle hint of "just solutions for the moral questions which arise in the conscience of the peoples." (*See Reading No. 36.*)

Wilhelm Marx: Dismissal and Return.   Meanwhile, the political climate on the domestic front was normal —that is, chaotic. From 1926 to 1928 the fulcrum of political power in the Republic was Wilhelm Marx (1863-1946), jurist and prominent leader of the Center party. Marx held the chancellorship under four cabinets: November-June, 1924; June 1924—January 1925; May 1926—January 1927; and January 1927—June 1928.

In early January 1927 the Social Democrats, excluded from the cabinet, attacked the government because it allowed "the financing of the *Reichswehr* by Russia," and permitted the Army's connection with industrial magnates and Rightist groups. On January 29, 1927, joined by the German Nationalists, the Social Democrats introduced a motion of no-confidence in the *Reichstag* and won it by a vote of 249 to 171. Marx was dismissed as chancellor. The Social Democrats had their parliamentary victory, but the German Nationalists were the ones to profit. And in the reshuffle which brought German Nationalists into the cabinet, Marx remained as chancellor.

Bringing German Nationalists into the cabinet was a grievous blow to the Republic. For years these harsh enemies of the Republic had obstructed Stresemann's policy of reconciliation with the Allies. These were precarious times for German democrats.

Chancellor Marx and Foreign Minister Stresemann did their best to work with the German Nationalists. It was not easy. Rightist agitators accused Stresemann of being "a common blackguard" who "could be bought." Matters were not helped when, on September 18, 1927, President Hindenburg took part in the Tannenberg National Monument ceremony in East Prussia, commemorating the German victory over the Russians in August 1914. The old field marshal delivered an address in which he revived the war-guilt issue by proclaiming Germany's innocence. (*See Reading No. 37.*) No one doubted Hindenburg's right to express his private opinion on so dangerous a subject, but he was speaking as president of Germany. Moreover, from Holland came a telegram from the former Kaiser signed "William, Emperor and King." The Hohenzollern, as if he were still on the royal throne, was speaking to his faithful paladin. People began talking about "this fool's paradise of a Republic."

In the elections of May 20, 1928, the Social Democrats increased the number of their seats in the *Reichstag* from 131 to 152. At the same time there was a rise in Communist delegates from 45 to 54. For the first time since 1920 a Social Democrat, Herman Müller, became chancellor.

Stresemann continued to hold the office of foreign minister. He played an important role in the negotiations leading to the Kellogg-Briand pact, signed on August 27, 1928 by representatives of fifteen powers. The contracting parties agreed "that the settlement of all disputes or conflicts of whatever nature or of whatever origin they may be, which may arise among them, shall never be sought except by pacific means." Stresemann, although seriously ill at the time, made the trip to Paris to sign the pact. He was received by the populace with cries of *"Vive Stresemann!"* These were the same people who, nine years earlier, had turned their backs on the German plenipotentiaries at the peace conference.

The Young Plan, 1929. Between 1924 and 1929 Germany had climbed from the pit of despair to the top level of the world's nations. It was a spectacular recovery, due only in part to the influx of foreign funds. The Germans went to work with tremendous zeal. They built new factories, roads, railways, and canals, and extended telephone and telegraph services. After turning large quantities of rolling stock and locomotives over to the Allies in the form of reparations, they proceeded diligently and intelligently to build larger freight cars and more powerful locomotives. Those merchant ships given to the Allies were replaced by new ones with more modern equipment. By 1929 Germany's industrial power was greater than that of any other Continental country.

During the prosperous years the Germans had promptly met their reparations annuities fixed under the Dawes Plan. They were, however, dissatisfied with the provisional nature of the settlement, which they regarded as only a stopgap to meet a crisis. Stresemann was anxious to effect a new settlement before the "standard" annuity payment in 1928-1929 would put German liability at an impossible rate. At his urging, representatives of the Powers met privately in Geneva in September 1928 to seek a "complete and final" settlement of the reparations problem.

As a result, the Young Committee, led by the American financier Owen D. Young, convened early in 1929 and formulated a series of recommendations: (1) The old Dawes Transfer Committee was abolished and Germany herself was required not only to collect the reparations payments but also to transfer them to the Allies. (2) A new indemnity bill was set at $8,032,500,000 to be paid over a period of fifty-eight and a half years. (The actual payments, which included interest at 5½ per cent, were to total approximately 29 billion dollars from 1928 to 1988). (3) The average annuities for the first thirty-seven years were placed at 511 million dollars; the remaining twenty-two annuities were to average 390 million dollars. (4) The unconditional or unpostponable part of each annuity was set at 162 million dollars, of which France was to receive three-fourths. (5) A new Bank for International Settlements would act as trustee for the creditor powers, distribute reparations payments, and "furnish the world of international commerce with important facilities hitherto lacking."

The Young Plan was received well everywhere but inside Germany. Unconvinced of their war guilt, Germans asked why they would have to continue payments for fifty-eight and a half years until 1988. Why should generations yet unborn be saddled with the debts of their elders? Dr. Schacht resigned in protest as head of the Reichsbank. (*See Reading No. 38.*) German Nationalists, Nazis, and Communists joined in denouncing the Young Plan. Nevertheless, the *Reichstag* voted acceptance, and on March 13, 1930, President Hindenburg signed the bills. The Bank for International Settlement opened its offices at Basel. But before the first payment was due under the Young Plan there came unmistakable signs of an economic blizzard.

— 7 —

CULTURE IN THE
RELUCTANT REPUBLIC

The Era of Disenchantment. The Germans went to war in 1914 in an outburst of wild enthusiasm. The conflict was supposed to have been short and triumphant. But then came blockade, mounting casualty lists, endless disappointment, and finally the ignominy of defeat. The Weimar Republic was launched in a sea of pessimism and disillusionment. This note of futility was captured in the literature of the postwar period. The public turned eagerly to realistic accounts of the brutality and devastation of war. Erich Maria Remarque's novels, *All Quiet on the Western Front* (1929) and *The Road Back* (1931), were sensational best sellers.

Germany's great poetic genius, the sensitive and imaginative Rainer Maria Rilke (1875-1926), was still alive to carry on his creative work. He was impressed with neither the German Revolution nor the Weimar Republic, for he saw no conversion, no change of heart in the German people. (*See Reading No. 39.*) Disgusted by the gross materialism and rampant militarism of his native land, he sought refuge in a purely esthetic life. He spent his last years in Switzerland. He would detach himself from the universe in order to see as a spectator the greatness of God and the puniness of man. Gerhart Hauptmann (1862-1946), dramatist, novelist, and poet, revered author of *The Weavers,* was already affected by the new mood of weariness, and produced little. Overwhelmed by an increasing sense of nationalism, Hauptmann submitted to the Nazi regime, thereby ending a distinguished career.

The Liberal Literary School.   Liberal and reactionary literary trends clashed head on. Those who accepted the Republic were delighted by the possibility of free expression in an open society. Liberal writers were opposed to the nationalism and militarism of the Wilhelmian era. Some were influenced by Freudian psychology, others by the literary experimentation of James Joyce. Heinrich Mann (1871-1950), novelist of the middle class, became president of the writers' section of the Prussian Academy of Arts. In a popular trilogy, distinguished by psychological insight and biting social criticism, he described German life as it existed in the regime of William II. Arnold Zweig (1887———), wrote a popular novel, *Der Streit um den Sergeanten Grischa* (*The Case of Sergeant Grischa*) (1927), which decried the suppression of the individual in wartime.

The case of Thomas Mann (1875-1955), the younger brother of Heinrich Mann, was unique. He had already established his fame with the publication in 1900 of *Buddenbrooks,* a saga of the gradual decay of a Lübeck merchant family through four generations. In 1914 Thomas Mann was engulfed in the wave of emotional patriotism. "The military spirit," he said in an oft-quoted passage, "is akin to the spirit of art. How the hearts of our poets were immediately ablaze, once war was declared! German militarism is the manifestation of German morality." This was nineteenth-century romanticism of the Richard Wagner variety. Mann realized his error after the war, when he became a passionate defender of the Weimar democracy. In his best-known novel, *The Magic Mountain* (1924), Mann tells how his hero, weakened by tuberculosis, attempted to discover himself and the meaning of life. It was a literary expression of Mann's own conversion to advocacy of the open society. After the advent of National Socialism, he went into voluntary exile and remained abroad until his death. Again and again he attacked the Nazi regime as a reversion to barbarism.

Proletarian Literature.   Proletarian literature flourished in the Weimar days. Bertold Brecht (1898-1956), novelist, playwright, and ballad writer, pioneered a type of "epic theatre" designed to arouse political passions in the spectator. His *Dreigroschenoper* (*Three-Penny Opera*), with music by Kurt Weill (1928), was an enormous success. Others, including Oskar Maria Graf, Theodor Plivier, and Ernst Toller, similarly attacked the impersonal state and directed shafts of ridicule at capitalism. Contemptuous of the bourgeoisie, these radical writers called for an end to the Weimar Republic and for the inauguration of a proletarian state.

Added to the proletarian critics was a small group of pacifists led by Carl von Ossietzky, who attacked the still flourishing Prussianism and militarism. The pacifists had no political aims—they merely abhorred war as evil cannibalism.

Reactionary Literary Enemies of the Republic. On the Right were those reactionary literary voices which detested the innovators. The rightists denounced liberal and proletarian writers as tools of Moscow who were responsible for the collapse of the German mind. Some were fanatical anti-Semites who were certain that Germany's dark days were the result of "Jewish ideals." All denounced the Weimar Republic as a vicious fraud perpetrated on the German people.

Among the Rightist literati was the poet Stefan George (1868-1933), founder of the *Blätter für die Kunst,* designed to reform the German language. He gathered around him an exclusive literary circle called the *George-Kreis,* which criticized the "decadent mass culture" and the "disintegrative democratic socialism" of the Weimar Republic. An advocate of symbolism, George called for an élite group to guide Germany to her rightful high place in civilization. One day, he predicted, there would appear a new Siegfried whose sword would lead Germans back to the days of pristine glory. His vision did not include a mustached Siegfried with a raucous rooster voice.

Among the critics of the Weimar Republic was Oswald Spengler (1880-1936), scientist and historical philosopher, author of *The Decline of the West* (1918-1923). A pessimist, Spengler held that each of the world cultures emerged independently of the others, achieved its climax, declined, and fell, in ever-repeating cycles—spring, summer, fall, and winter. All Europe was in decline and destined to die. In a later book, *Jahre der Entscheidung* (*Years of Decision*) (1933), Spengler urged European resurgence based on Prusso-German leadership. He spoke of Prussian youth as "Roman in its pride to serve, in the humility to command, demanding not rights from others but duties from oneself, all without exception, without distinction, to fulfill a destiny they feel within themselves." He had sympathetic admiration for the aristocratic warrior. He recommended a "Prussian Socialism," which differed only in degree from the National Socialism of Adolf Hitler. His neo-romanticism, clothed in a highly personalized jargon (*"makromosmus";* "Apollinian, Faustian, and Magian soul"; "soul-image"; "life-feeling"; "nature-knowledge"), struck a responsive chord among fuzzy-minded Germans.

The new pacifism was more than matched by a revival of jingoism and chauvinism. The defeat had been bitter, but it was not long before voices in praise of war were revived. On the one side there was denunciation of war and all its concomitants, on the other side came paeans praising war as a cleansing process of the human soul. (*See Reading No. 40.*)

Symptomatic of the Republic's difficulties was the rise of racialism, a kind of super-romanticism which edged into irrationalism. Still alive and preaching the doctrine of Nordic Teutonism was Houston Stewart Chamberlain (1855-1927), son of a British admiral. Born at Southsea, Chamberlain left England, married a daughter of Richard Wagner, and became a naturalized German. His admiration for all things German was coupled with an equally intense hatred for anything concerned with his native land. The entrance of the Teutonic "race," into history, he said, formed an opposing force to the diminutive but influential "race" of Jews. "To this day these two powers—Jews and Teutonic races—stand, wherever the recent spread of the Chaos has not blurred their features, now as friendly, now as hostile, but always as alien forces face to face." Chamberlain argued that all achievements in science, industry, political economy, and art were stimulated and propelled by the Teutonic race. The nineteenth century, he said, rested upon a secure Teutonic foundation, for it saw Teutonic blood "in its greatest purity." The Jews were a "community of blood" dedicated to the mission of controlling the world and enslaving all non-Jews. "Christ did not have a single drop of genuinely Jewish blood in his veins."

This sort of irrationalism would deserve little attention except that it took hold and became a kind of secular religion. Nowhere in *Mein Kampf* did Hitler mention Chamberlain by name, but he was, nevertheless, a disciple of the renegade Englishman.

Followers of Chamberlain were the forerunners of the Nazi revolution. Among them was Alfred Rosenberg (1893-1946), who later became Hitler's party philosopher and the *Fuehrer* of Nazi intellectualism. Moody, maudlin, egocentric, Rosenberg wrote *The Myth of the Twentieth Century* (*see Reading No. 41*), in effect a restatement of the Chamberlain thesis of race superiority. Rosenberg's first concern was a "scientific" justification for the Nazi blood myth. "The *Mythus* is the Mythus of the Blood, which, under the sign of the Swastika, released the World Revolution. It is the Awakening of the Soul of the Race, which, after a period of long slumber, victoriously put an end to the racial chaos." The real Christ, said Rosenberg, was an Amorite, aggressive, courageous, a man of true Nordic character, a revolutionist who opposed the Jewish and Roman systems with sword in hand, "bringing not peace but war."

Others, including Hans F. K. Günther, Friedrich Lenz, Eugen Fischer, and Hans Grimm, wrote in similar vein, seeking to find a mystical relationship between ethnic culture and the German soil. George Bernard Shaw called this racialist ideology "pernicious nonsense." Yet, this absurd balderdash has historical importance. It helped unify Germans in their opposition to the Weimar Republic. It gave them a feeling of ego-enhancement, increased status, and self-confidence. It was deadly serious and it helped prepare the way for Hitler.

Ferment in the Arts. There was similar agitation in music, painting, and architecture, and on the stage. The musical giant, Richard Strauss (1864-1949), was still alive, but his techniques had become repetitive and his invention dry. Arnold Schoenberg (1874-1951) made use of speech-song, disintegrated tonality, and twelve-note music, thereby stimulating concert-hall riots. Alban Berg (1885-1935), pupil of Schoenberg, made use of the twelve-note system in his opera, *Wozzeck*. Traditional German music remained on a high level of achievement. Annual Wagnerian festivals were held at Bayreuth under the direction of Siegfried Wagner, son of the composer.

German artists turned to expressionism, freely expressing their inner, or subjective, emotions and sensations. Proletarian artists devoted their efforts to exposés of the "ruling class." George Grosz revealed sharp social criticism in his striking drawings, and Käthe Kollwitz showed empathy for the miserable masses in her charcoal portraits. Walther Gropius's experimental *Bauhaus* in Dessau, stressing simple structural concepts, influenced the development of architecture everywhere. The theater was enlivened by the talent of Max Reinhardt, who employed the apron-stage and other devices to establish intimacy with audiences. The motion picture industry set a standard for the world with films featuring Emil Jannings, Marlene Dietrich, and Erich von Stroheim.

The Agitation of Escapism. These artistic tendencies in Germany reflected a similar world-wide pattern after the war. Those Germans who lived in small villages were unaffected by the new trends, but the industrialized urban society was suffused with commotion, glow, and excitement. Germans joined the jazz-age madness rampant throughout the whole world in the 1920's. Berlin became one of the most dissolute cities of modern times, with its round-the-clock bohemian activity, its absorption with sex, its desperate retreat from boredom. Puritanical minds of the lower middle class were appalled and angered by what they called either "Americanization" or "the Bolshevization of culture." These people turned with relief to the asceticism and glittering promises of Adolf Hitler.

— 8 —

DEATH AGONY: THE TWILIGHT OF GERMAN DEMOCRACY, 1929-1933

The Great Depression.   Germany's prosperity lasted only from 1925 to 1929. Her economic health was, to a great extent, the result of huge loans from abroad, especially from the United States. Closely geared to the world economy, she was the first country to be affected when it shifted into imbalance. A critical stage started when the industrial powers, the United States, Britain, and France, began to close their doors to foreign goods. The Hawley-Smoot Act, passed by the United States Congress in 1930, imposed higher tariffs on 890 categories of imports. This was followed by the creation of the British system of imperial preference and a network of preferential trade agreements in the French Empire. The Germans replied by increasing their own tariffs as much as 100 per cent.

Weimar Germany began to feel the effects of a tightening economy in early 1929. Revenues declined precipitously. Soon the national treasury was almost empty. Prices and wages sank. Conditions became worse during the rest of the year 1929. The crash of the New York stock exchange in October 1929, with repercussions all over the world, turned the German recession into a disaster of major proportions. The Depression hit Germany with thunderous impact. Countless businesses and industries went bankrupt, and foreclosures took place every day. Income began to decline to the danger point. The loss of foreign credit and the sudden recall of short-term American loans were blows from which the German economy could not recover. The Weimar Republic was on the brink of disaster.

Worst of all was the effect on the working population. Unemployment had not been a problem during the prosperous years from 1925 to 1929, but in early 1929 there were 2,019,000 jobless. By 1930 the figure rose to 3,483,000; in 1931 it was 4,409,000; and in 1932 it was more than 6 million, more than in all other European states combined. By the end of 1932 nearly half of Germany's labor force was jobless. It was a catastrophic situation. The unemployment-insurance system, unfortunately designed to handle short-term, small-scale unemployment, all but collapsed. Hungry men wandered through the streets wondering how they could care for their families. Those who had jobs were forced to accept reduced rates of pay. Others were destitute or had to depend on the dole. People deliberately sought arrest so that they might get something to eat in prison. (*See Reading No. 42.*)

Through their unions the workers had small unemployment insurance payments to keep them going for a time. But the lower middle class—shopkeepers, intellectuals, professional people—was hard hit. Unorganized, bewildered by economic forces they did not understand, angered by the loss of their self-respect, the little people of Germany were in a desperate situation. They had nothing to which to look forward except the prospect of steady deterioration. This was the class which became psychologically ripe for the blandishments of Adolf Hitler. Together with the proletariat, the middle class tried to escape from economic chaos by seeking salvation in a dictatorship. This was by no means an exclusively German phenomenon. The German people were to find the cure considerably worse than the disease.

Political Recoil: Heinrich Brüning. The Social Democrats had the unfortunate task of trying to steer the country through stormy economic waters. Nationalist agitators began to demand the reduction of unemployment benefits, which they held to be responsible for the country's financial troubles. Chancellor Herman Müller, Social Democrat, whose cabinet had been in power since

June 1928, categorically refused to lower the dole. The parliamentary battle over this issue lasted through 1929 into 1930, at the time when another conflict over the acceptance of the Young plan was taking place. Stresemann, still foreign minister, was concerned that these political battles might endanger his foreign policy. Seriously ill, he spent the last day of his life, October 2, 1929, pleading with his own People's party to follow the path of moderation and not hinder the Social Democrats in their opposition to lower unemployment payments. The next day, after a stroke, Stresemann died. Without his moderating influence, the situation grew worse. On March 27, 1930, following acceptance of the Young Plan, Chancellor Müller resigned.

In choosing a successor to Müller, President Hindenburg was influenced by General Kurt von Schleicher (1882-1934), a member of the Prussian nobility, who had been appointed to the staff of the quartermaster-general during the war and who had held staff posts throughout the conflict. A protégé of General Groener, Schleicher had helped create the foundations for the new *Reichswehr*. A master of political intrigue, he had joined the so-called palace camarilla, which included, among others, Oskar von Hindenburg, influential son of the old president. For the chancellorship Schleicher recommended Heinrich Brüning (1884-   ), an economist who in 1929 had been elected parliamentary leader of the Catholic Center party. Brüning, a front fighter in the war, had been undecided after the conflict whether to go into politics or, because he was a devout Catholic, enter the religious life. A cold, soft-spoken man, almost completely devoid of political charm, he regarded his weapons as logic and statistics rather than eloquence or political chicanery. He was quite willing to rule by presidential decree, a bad omen for the Republic. His cabinet, which contained no Social Democrats, was weighted heavily to the Right.

Brüning presented his program to the *Reichstag* on April 1, 1930. In this first appearance before the house he was greeted with cries of "Hunger chancellor!" Unmoved, he presented a constructive program of economic retrenchment. To appease the Nationalists, he supported the *Osthilfe*, a program of financial help for the large landowners in the east, a subject close to the heart of President Hindenburg. In foreign policy, Brüning called for: (1) fulfillment of existing agreements; (2) close relations with those states friendly to Germany; and (3) encouragement of international cooperation, especially in the economic field, to help Germany in her current economic difficulties. With the support of the Nationalists, the Communists' move of no-confidence was defeated by a vote of 253 to 187.

Relations between chancellor and *Reichstag* quickly degenerated. In mid-July, Brüning demanded that the *Reichstag* approve his fiscal policy and pass a balanced budget. He intimated that otherwise he was ready to rule by presidential decree. Hindenburg supported his chancellor by promising use of Article 48. When, on July 16, 1930, a coalition of Communists, Social Democrats, Nationalists, and National Socialists defeated several governmental projects, Brüning decreed his program as an emergency measure. The *Reichstag*, by a majority of only fifteen votes, countered with a demand for withdrawal of the presidential edicts. Hindenburg then signed a decree dissolving the *Reichstag* and setting September 14, 1930 as the date for new elections. From that moment on Germany hardly had a parliamentary system.

The Growing Nazi Threat. Meanwhile, Hitler was making political capital out of the current depression. He stepped up the Nazi proaganda drive. (*See Readings Nos. 43 and 44.*) There were political successes. In April 1930, Nazis were appointed to leading positions in the police administration of Thuringia. In the elections in Saxony on June 22, 1930, the Nazis increased their strength in the Diet from five to fourteen, and became the second strongest party in Saxony. As the economic crisis worsened in the summer of 1930, Nazi brownshirts and Communists fought pitched battles in Berlin. Both sides promised bread and jobs for their followers. In carefully timed speeches, Hitler appealed to the pride of his listeners. He glorified the German "race" and promised a great future to people mired in economic quicksand. Germans of all classes and parties seemed to be hypnotized by the pudgy little Austrian with the husky voice. Gradually, the Nazis began to win the propaganda struggle and the battle of the streets.

Outside Germany there was little understanding of what was happening to the Weimar Republic. Few observers understood that it was on the verge of collapse. Such anti-Germans as Georges Clemenceau, wartime premier of France, worried less about Hitler than about the prospect of Germany re-arming. (*See Reading No. 45.*)

The *Reichstag* Elections of 1930.   The fifth national election campaign was loud, boisterous, and ferocious. Some 35 million voters went to the polls on September 14, 1930. The results were ominous. The Social Democrats managed to retain their position as the largest party in the *Reichstag,* but they lost a number of seats and now had 143 deputies. The extremists on both sides made huge gains. The Communists received 4,587,000 votes, an increase of forty per cent, and jumped from 54 to 77 seats. The great sensation of the day was the showing of the Nazis, who polled almost six and a half million votes, and increased their representation from 12 to 107. They now had the second largest party in the *Reichstag.* A shock of amazement reverberated throughout Germany with this landslide Nazi victory. It was a miserable day for the Weimar Republic.

Accelerated Crisis: The Harzburg Front.   The winter of 1930-1931 saw a continued financial crisis. Brüning was faced with an almost impossible task—to solve the economic chaos and at the same time appease enough political factions in order to remain in power. He did what he could to relieve the financial distress. At the same time he tried to reach some sort of understanding with the rapidly rising Nazis. But he was fundamentally anti-Nazi and was not impressed with Hitler's plans for the future.

On October 11, 1931, in the little town of Harzburg in Brunswick, a great conclave of parties of the Right convened for the purpose of uniting to oust Brüning and set up "a truly national government." In this unique gathering were represented the Nationalists, Pan-Germans, generals and admirals, spokesmen for heavy industry, the *Stahlhelm,* Junkers, and Nazis. Among the personalities

present were Alfred Hugenberg, leader of the Nationalists; Fritz Thyssen, director of the United Steel Works;
Franz Seldte, head of the *Stahlhelm;* Hjalmar Schacht;
and Adolf Hitler. Hitler attained some respectability by
being included among the gathering of ultra-Rightists.
Hugenberg, demanding that Germany be saved from the
Bolshevik peril and from national bankruptcy, called for
Brüning's resignation and for new elections. Hitler, speaking along similar lines, predicted that Germany would
turn either to Bolshevism or to nationalism. The Harzburg front was a powerful combination. It had money,
as well as influence, and, with Hitler and his Nazis, it
had mass support. It was able to muster more political
strength than its rival—organized labor. Between the
Harzburg front and political control stood only the vener-
able President Hindenburg, who could keep a minority
cabinet in power as long as he invoked the authority of
Article 48.

Hitler's Düsseldorf Speech.   On January 27, 1932,
Hitler was invited to Düsseldorf, the capital of the German steel industry, to address the Industry Club, the
entire body of Rhenish-Westphalian industrialists. It was
the first time that most German industrialists had met
Hitler, and their reception was cool and reserved. But
the Nazi leader recognized an opportunity when he saw
it. For two and a half hours he harangued the assembled
coal and steel barons. (*See Reading No. 46.*) In one of
the shrewdest speeches of his life, he pulled out every
one of the stock ideas on which he had built his propaganda. He wanted big business to know that he and his
Nazis could be trusted. All that propaganda about *Zins-
knechtschaft* ("slavery of interest") was just so much
electioneering rubbish, and the industrialists need not
take it seriously. It was a virtuoso performance. Hitler
denounced democracy. He defended private property. He
dwelt on the Red menace. He praised National Socialism, and shouted that he would lead the Germans
back to faith and ideals.

When Hitler finished his oration, the audience rose
and cheered him enthusiastically. True, this loud little
man was uncouth and lacking in tone, tact, and taste, but
he had some right ideas. It was an important day in the

history of Germany: the industrialists had their champion to protect them against the surge of radicalism, against Communism and the trade unions. On his part, Hitler now had access to the industrialists' purse strings. From then on, large contributions from heavy industry began to flow into the Nazi treasury. The goal of power was now in sight for Hitler.

Re-election of Hindenburg. In early 1932, in the midst of the severe political and economic crises, Hindenburg's presidential term drew to a close. The field marshal was now eighty-four years old and declining in both physical and mental health. With weak eyesight, he grew ever more dependent upon his son, Oskar, who acted as his secretary. It was a standing joke that anyone in his entourage who brought sandwiches for lunch was cautioned to destroy the paper wrappers, because if left around they would be signed by the old man. Hindenburg became highly susceptible to the influence of the camarilla surrounding him, particularly by "his gray eminence," General Schleicher. Although reluctant to run for another term, the president allowed himself to be persuaded by Schleicher to stand again for election. Ironically, Hindenburg had been a candidate of the conservatives in 1925, but now he was supported by defenders of the Republic against attacks from the Right.

On the first ballot Hindenburg polled 18,650,730 votes (49.6 per cent), Hitler 11,339,285 (30.1 per cent), the Communist, Thälmann 4,983,197 (13 per cent), and Düsterberg, Nationalist, 2,558,000 (6.8 per cent). Again, as in 1925, because no candidate had won a majority of the votes, a second ballot was required. In the new ballot, held a month later, Hindenburg received 19,359,-635 votes (53 per cent), Hitler 13,418,051 (26.8 per cent), and Thälmann 3,796,655 (10.2 per cent). This time the Nationalist *Stahlhelm* threw its votes to Hitler, but the gesture was not enough to elect him. An indication of a lack of interest was the fact that a million fewer voters came to the polls.

Hindenburg's election was due in some measure to support given him by Brüning. Yet, within a few weeks, in an extraordinary act of political ingratitude, the old man forced the resignation of his loyal chancellor. Oskar Hindenburg, his cronies, and the East Elbian landlords played on the president's fears. They convinced him that Brüning, his trusted chancellor, had sold out to the Bolsheviks by supporting "Communist trade union activities." The old man was infuriated when he learned that Brüning had proposed a partial expropriation of East Prussian estates so that peasants could settle on them.

There was a personal issue involved here. On October 2, 1927, on his eightieth birthday, Hindenburg had been presented with an estate called Neudeck in East Prussia, which had once been the ancestral property of his family. The estate was purchased by public subscription and given to the president with the compliments and gratitude of the nation. But the idea of making Hindenburg a member of the landholding class had come from the Junker landowners, who feared that the *Reichstag* might split up their estates. It worked. Hindenburg became an obstacle in the way of land reform.

The von Papen Interlude. On May 31, 1932, the day after Brüning's resignation, Hindenburg, again on the advice of Schleicher, named Franz von Papen as chancellor. A Catholic aristocrat from Westphalia, Papen had been military attaché in the United States at the start of World War I, but was forced to leave because of his complicity in plots to blow up American munitions factories. Later he was chief of the general staff of the Turkish army in Palestine. In Berlin he played an important role in the *Herrenklub,* a social club whose members considered themselves to be among the international élite. André François-Poncet, the French ambassador, reported that both Papen's friends and enemies considered him to be a superficial, confused thinker and an ambitious and scheming intriguer. "The Devil in top hat" was the judgment of one observer.

Papen named a "cabinet of barons" composed of conservative Junkers, Rhineland industrialists, and military leaders, a combination he thought would keep the upstart Hitler out of power. Included in the cabinet were Schleicher as minister of defense, Baron Konstantin von Neurath at the foreign office, and Count Lutz Schwerin-Krosigk at the ministry of finance. Three days after assuming his office Papen dissolved the *Reichstag*. A week later, honoring the promise he had made to Hitler, he lifted the ban against the Nazi storm-troopers (S.A.) and the élite corps (S.S.). Instead of striking at Nazis and Communists, who were fighting pitched battles in the streets, Papen deposed the Social Democratic premier of Prussia, Otto Braun, on the ground that Braun had been unable to maintain the peace. It was an unconstitutional move, smacking of dictatorial temper, but the Social Democrats seemed to be paralyzed, and did nothing. The Communists threatened a strike, but they got no support from the Social Democrats, who hated the Communists even more than they hated the Nazis.

The election campaign of July 31, 1932 was as violent as usual. By now dubbed "Adolf Légalité" because he had promised to obtain power legally, Hitler pushed his raucous campaign into every corner of Germany. It was an effective circus. When the votes were counted there was another National Socialist landslide. The Nazis polled 13,700,000 votes with 230 seats in the *Reichstag*, more than double their previous representation, but they still had no absolute majority. The Communists also made some gains, winning 89 seats, some at the expense of the Social Democrats.

Hitler was the man of the hour. It became clear that there could not be any kind of government in Germany without the participation of the National Socialists, the largest party in the country. As chancellor, Papen could count on only two parties, the Nationalists and the People's party, which together could muster only 44 votes in the *Reichstag*.

During the summer and fall of 1932, Papen, Schleicher, and Hitler indulged in a Byzantine jockeying for power. Hitler brusquely rejected Papen's offer of the vice-chancellorship. He would have all or nothing. When, on August 13, 1932, Hindenburg offered Hitler a place in the cabinet headed by Papen, the Nazi *Führer* again refused. (*See Reading No. 47.*) Papen then shifted his tactics. He dissolved the *Reichstag* and called for new elections, expecting that the results would show a weakening of the Nazis. He was right, up to a point. In the November elections of 1932, Hitler lost some two million votes and 34 seats in the *Reichstag*. At least some of the public had been alienated by the excesses of Nazi bully boys. There was a sense of relief among the democratic elements. But Hitler had no intention of fading away.

From Schleicher to Hitler. On November 17, 1932, Papen offered his resignation with the hope that Hindenburg would recall him to the chancellorship. Once more the president summoned Hitler and offered him the post, but again Hitler demanded full powers, and once more Hindenburg refused. On December 2, 1932, Schleicher, who had been instrumental in intrigues leading to the making and the fall of cabinets, was himself called to the post. Schleicher decided that he must stop Hitler's drive for power. He worked out a plan to bring together Gregor Strasser's Left wing of the Nazi party and several bourgeois leaders and trade-union elements into a coalition which would withstand Hitler. The latter, cannily sensing Strasser's defection, stripped him of his offices and threw him out of the party. Schleicher's scheme for a working coalition collapsed. For his decision he was to pay with his life in the Nazi blood purge of 1934.

Papen and Schleicher, both furious at what they regarded their betrayal by Hitler, met secretly in Cologne on January 4, 1933, at the home of the banker Kurt von Schroeder. Settling their old feud, the two revived the Harzburg front. Again, money began to pour into the Nazi coffers, by this time almost dry. Schleicher, sensing that his only hope was to dissolve the *Reichstag* and establish a military dictatorship, asked Hindenburg to sign a decree of dissolution. Hindenburg, worried about the constitutionality of the move, refused.

Meanwhile, the wily Papen began to spin a web. His plan was to convince Hitler, on the one hand, to accept the chancellorship in a coalition cabinet, and on the other, to persuade Hindenburg that, with himself as vice-chancellor, he could prevent a Nazi dictatorship. The old man had little use for "this lance corporal" and he was most reluctant to call the Nazi leader to the chancellorship. But when Papen convinced him that civil war was the only alternative, Hindenburg gave in. Additional explanations have been presented as to why Hindenburg bowed to the detested Nazi. One point of view holds that the aged president feared that the Nazis would depose him by a *coup d'état*. Others argue that the president was blackmailed by a Nazi threat to bring into the open the scandal of the *Osthilfe*,[1] which Hindenburg had supported. No matter what the interpretation, Hitler had driven to power under a thin veneer of legality.

Schleicher resigned on January 28, 1933. (*See Reading No. 48.*) Shortly after noon on January 30, 1933, a new government was announced with Hitler as chancellor and Papen as vice-chancellor. (*See Reading No. 49.*) On that evening, the impassive old president and a beaming Hitler reviewed a torchlight procession of enthusiastic Nazis from a window in the *Wilhelmstrasse*. The Weimar Republic had committed suicide; the German democracy was now dead. Exactly a year later the *Reich* was reorganized into a dictatorship. (*See Reading No. 50.*)

[1] *Osthilfe*, a program of eastern aid, a rescue operation undertaken by the government to assist the agricultural interests of the eastern German provinces, which were suffering distress in part because of their separation from Germany by the Polish Corridor.

— 9 —

POSTSCRIPT:
THE TRAGEDY OF HISTORY

The Child of Defeat. Although they were enduring hunger, privation, and misery, the German people hoped for a miracle of victory until the closing months of World War I. They lived in a curious dream world. Everything would straighten itself out. They were sure that eventually German streets would resound with cries of joy and the ringing of bells. The official communiqués still referred to German victories on the battlefields. Not a square inch of German territory had been invaded by the enemy.

Then, seemingly overnight, came the heartbreaking news of defeat. William II was thrust aside and the Republic was proclaimed. The new government was tarnished from its very beginning with the odium and odor of frustration. The victorious Allies occupied German territory; war prisoners were not sent home; the naval blockade was maintained. All this was fiercely resented, and all of it was associated in the German mind with the Weimar Republic, the illegitimate child of defeat.

The new Republic was born without adequate planning or preparation, almost as an afterthought. The architects of Weimar worked in a hurry to produce a government which they believed would be regarded with favor by the Allies and which would assure them an easier peace. There was little mass support. If it is true that a democracy can be successful only if it is wanted by the people, then the German democracy was doomed from its very start. Most Germans saw the Weimar Republic as a kind of artificial creation, a stopgap, care-taker government pending recall of the Hohenzollerns. They were much less interested in political democracy than in their own day-to-day problems. From the days of its origin the Weimar Republic was unwanted and un-loved. It died unhonored and unsung.

The basic weakness of the Weimar Republic was the same one that burdened every other political movement in German history—the feebleness of the German brand of liberalism. It was this fragility that led to the failure of 1848. There was always a great disparity between the political aspirations of German leaders and the mass sup-port and actual influence they commanded. In 1848 it had seemed that the streams of rationalism—liberalism, democracy, social contract, egalitarianism, tolerance, and constitutionalism—were converging at long last in a com-mon stream. For the first time in their history the German people had an opportunity to determine their own destiny. But when the wave of revolution receded, liberal na-tionalism was buried in its dregs and the Prusso-German symbiosis was triumphant.

In 1919 came another opportunity. But again there were too few democratically minded people, and once again those who did profess liberal democracy diluted its content until it became all but unrecognizable. It was a Republic without republicans: too few Germans pre-ferred the democratic way of life.

Added to this fundamental weakness inside Germany was critical misunderstanding from the outside. Not only were the Germans ill-prepared for an advanced form of democracy, but the triumphant Allies showed little sym-pathy for the Weimar Republic. In the heat of war propaganda, the Allies had made a careful distinction between the German people and their reactionary rulers. That discrimination was dropped once the war was won. Germans, who believed that they had laid down their arms on the basis of the Wilsonian Fourteen Points, cried that they had been victimized in a gigantic hoax. They complained that they had placed their trust in Allied promises and as a reward they had been treated ignominiously.

The Weimar Republic, constructed on a weak frame, unsupported by public opinion, lacking help from the outside, was unable to weather the storms of opposition from both Right and Left. It was betrayed by friends and foes alike. It was not strong enough to withstand political chaos, economic trials, social distress, and psychological anxiety. What had started out as a bold experiment in democracy, degenerated into the nightmare of Hitlerism.

Part II

READINGS

— Reading No. 1 —

THE FIRST GERMAN PEACE NOTE, OCTOBER 3, 1918 [1]

On October 6, 1918, a communication from Prince Max of Baden, chancellor of the German government, to the president of the United States, transmitted through the Swiss legation in Washington, requested steps for the restoration of peace.

↗   ↗   ↗

The German Government requests the President of the United States of America to take steps for the restoration of peace, to notify all belligerents of this request, and to invite them to delegate plenipotentiaries for the purpose of taking up negotiations. The German Government accepts, as a basis for the peace negotiations, the program laid down by the President of the United States in his message to Congress of January 8, 1918, and in his subsequent pronouncements, particularly in his address of September 27, 1918. In order to avoid further bloodshed the German Government requests to bring about the immediate conclusion of a general armistice on land, on water, and in the air.

MAX, Prince of Baden,
Imperial Chancellor

[1] United States Public Information Committee, *Official United States Bulletin,* October 9, 1918, Vol. II, No. 433.

— Reading No. 2 —

EBERT'S MANIFESTO, NOVEMBER 9, 1918 [2]

On the morning of November 9, 1918, Prince Max, with the understanding that a constituent assembly would be invoked, yielded his office as chancellor to Friedrich Ebert. The latter immediately issued a manifesto urging the country to remain tranquil.

FELLOW CITIZENS:

Prince Max of Baden, Reich chancellor up to now, with the consent of all the state secretaries, has turned over to me the task of carrying on the affairs of the Reich chancellor. I have in mind to form a government by consent of the parties and will give a public report on this shortly.

The new government will be a people's government. Its goal will be to bring peace to the German people as soon as possible, and to establish firmly the freedom which it has achieved.

Fellow Citizens: I ask you all for your support in the heavy tasks that await us. You know how seriously the war has threatened the sustenance of the people, the first basic condition for political life.

The political revolution should not interfere with the feeding of the population.

It must remain the first duty of all, both in the city and on the farms, not to hinder but rather to further the pro-

[2] Quoted in Koppel S. Pinson, *Modern Germany* (New York, 1954), p. 362. Courtesy of The Macmillan Company.

duction of food supplies and their transportation to the cities.

The want of food supplies means plunder and looting and suffering for all. The poorest will suffer most, the industrial workers will be hit hardest.

Whoever uses force to seize food supplies or other consumer needs or interferes with the means of transportation necessary for their distribution, sins heavily against the entire community.

Fellow Citizens! I implore you most urgently to leave the streets and maintain calm and order!

— Reading No. 3 —

PROCLAMATION OF THE GERMAN REPUBLIC, NOVEMBER 9, 1918 [3]

The proclamation of the German Republic marked a turn in German and European history. Philipp Scheidemann, who, along with Friedrich Ebert, was a leader of the German Majority Socialists, wrote a vivid account of what happened shortly after noon on November 9, 1918.

✦ ✦ ✦

On the morning of 9th November, 1918, the Reichstag was like an armed camp. Working men and soldiers were going in and out. Many bore arms. With Ebert, who had come from the Chancery to the Reichstag, and other friends, I sat hungry in the dining-hall. Thin, watery soup was the only thing to be had. . . .

Then a crowd of workers and soldiers rushed into the hall and made straight for our table.

Fifty of them yelled out at the same time, "Scheidemann, come along with us at once Philipp, you must come out and speak."

I refused; how many times had I not already spoken!

"You must, you must, if trouble is to be avoided. There are thousands upon thousands outside shouting for you to

[3] Philipp Scheidemann, *The Making of New Germany: Memoirs,* trans., J. E. Michell (New York, 1929), II, 261-263. Copyright by D. Appleton and Company. By permission of Appleton, Century, Crofts, Inc.

speak. Come along quick, Scheidemann! Liebknecht is already speaking from the balcony of the Schloss."

"Well, if I must."

"Come along now. You must."

Dozens urged it upon me, till I went off with them.

The main lobby presented a dramatic spectacle. Guns were piled up in stacks. From the courtyard the trampling and neighing of horses could be heard. In the hall thousands of hustling men seemed to be talking and shouting at the same time. We hurried away towards the reading-room. I intended to speak to the crowd from the window.

Those with me, right and left, pressed me to look at what was going on in the street. Between the Schloss and the Reichstag, so they said, masses of people were moving up and down.

"Liebknecht intends to proclaim the Soviet Republic!"

Now I clearly saw what was afoot. I knew his slogan—supreme authority for the Workers' and Soldiers' Councils. Germany to be therefore a Russian province, a branch of the Soviet? No, no, a thousand times no!

There was no doubt at all. The man who could bring along the "Bolshies" from the Schloss to the Reichstag or the Social Democrats from the Reichstag to the Schloss had won the day.

I saw the Russian folly staring me in the face—the Bolshevist tyranny, the substitute for the tyranny of the Czars! No, no, Germany should not have that on the top of all her other miseries.

I was already standing at the window. Many thousands of poor folk were trying to wave their hats and caps. The shouts of the crowds sounded like a mighty chorus. Then there was silence. I only said a few words, which were received with tremendous cheering.

"Workers and soldiers, frightful were those four years of war, ghastly the sacrifices the people made in blood and treasure. The cursed War is at an end. Murder has ceased. The fruits of war, want and misery, will burden us for years. The catastrophe we tried our best to avoid has not been spared us, because our proposals for peace by consent were rejected and we ourselves scorned and despised. The foes of an industrious people, the real foes in our midst, that have caused Germany's downfall, are silent and invisible. These were the warriors who stopped at home, promoting their demands for annexation, bitterly opposing any reform of the Constitution, and especially supporting the scandalous electoral system of Prussia. These foes are, it is to be hoped, gone for good. The Emperor has abdicated. He and his friends have decamped. The people have triumphed over them all along the line. Prince Max of Baden has handed over his office as Chancellor to Ebert. Our friend will form a Labour Government to which all Socialist Parties will belong. The new Government must not be hampered in their work for peace or their efforts for supplying food and work.

"Workmen and soldiers realize the historic importance of today. Miracles have happened. Long and incessant toil is before us. Everything for the people; everything by the people! Nothing must be done that brings dishonor to the Labour movement. Stand united and loyal, and be conscious of your duty. The old and rotten—the monarchy—has broken down. Long live the new! Long live the German Republic!"

Endless cheering broke out. Then the crowds began to move towards the Schloss. The Bolshevist wave that threatened to engulf Germany had spent its force. The German Republic had become a thing of life in the brains and hearts of the masses.

— Reading No. 4 —

PROCLAMATION OF
THE GOVERNMENT,
NOVEMBER 10, 1918 [4]

The proclamation of the Ebert council on November 10, 1918, designed to clarify the aims of the new government, was an event of far-reaching importance. A notable document, it signalized the attainment of goals long pursued by Socialists and liberals.

✓   ✓   ✓

To the German People!

The government created by the Revolution, the policy of which is purely Socialist, is setting itself the task of implementing the Socialistic program. With the full force of the law it now promulgates the following:

1. The "state of siege" is suspended.

2. The right of assembly and association is unrestricted, for officials as well as government workers.

3. Censorship does not exist. Censorship for theaters is lifted.

4. Freedom of speech and of the press is re-established.

5. Religious freedom is guaranteed. No one shall be forced to hold any particular religious views.

6. Amnesty is hereby granted for all political offenses. All such remaining punishable offenses are hereby revoked.

[4] Quoted in Johannes Hohlfeld (ed.), *Das Zeitalter Wilhelms*, II, 1890-1918 (Berlin and Munich, n.d.), III, 421-422. Courtesy of Giersch & Co. Translated by the editor.

7. The law concerning military service is revoked, subject to settlement of controversies still to be determined.

8. Regulations for servants are cancelled. Also the exceptional laws against farm workers.

Furthermore, ordinances, social and political, will be published shortly. At the latest on January 1, 1919, the 8-hour working day will come into effect. The government will do its utmost to provide work. A decree for the support of the unemployed is ready. It divides the costs among Reich, state, and community. In the matter of sickness insurance, the payments will be stretched beyond the 2500 mark point. Steps are being taken to insure a regular food supply.

Production will be maintained in all branches of the national economy. Property rights will be protected against infringement by private individuals.

All elections to public bodies are henceforward to be conducted according to equal, secret, direct, and universal suffrage, based on proportional representation, for all males and females from 20 years old. This electoral law applies to elections for the Constituent Assembly, concerning which further instructions will follow.

Berlin, November 12, 1919

EBERT   HAASE   SCHEIDEMANN   LANDSBERG
DITTMANN   BARTH

— Reading No. 5 —

THE TERMS OF THE ARMISTICE, NOVEMBER 11, 1918 [5]

At 5:00 A.M. on the morning of November 11, 1918, the armistice was signed by Marshal Ferdinand Foch, commander-in-chief of the Allied armies, with Admiral R. E. Wemyss, First Sea Lord of Great Britain, on the one hand, and the German plenipotentiaries on the other. The German representatives were Matthias Erzberger, German secretary of state, Count von Oberndorff, Major-General von Winterfeldt, and Captain Vanselow (German navy).

The New York Times *reported the event in these banner headlines:*

ARMISTICE SIGNED, END OF THE WAR!
BERLIN SEIZED BY REVOLUTIONISTS!
NEW CHANCELLOR BEGS FOR ORDER:
OUSTED KAISER FLEES TO HOLLAND

A summary of the terms of the armistice follows.

✓   ✓   ✓

1. Effective six hours after signing.
2. Immediate clearing of Belgium, France, Alsace-Lorraine, to be concluded within fourteen days. Any troops remaining in these areas to be interned or taken as prisoners of war.
3. Surrender of 5,000 cannon (chiefly heavy), 30,000 machine guns, 3,000 trench mortars, 2,000 planes.

[5] Official release by the German government, published in the *Kreuz-Zeitung*, November 11, 1918.

4. Evacuation of the left bank of the Rhine, Mayence, Coblenz, Cologne, occupied by the enemy to a radius of 30 kilometers deep.

5. On the right bank of the Rhine a neutral zone from 30 to 40 kilometers deep, evacuation within eleven days.

6. Nothing to be removed from the territory on the left bank of the Rhine, all factories, railroads, etc., to be left intact.

7. Surrender of 5,000 locomotives, 150,000 railway coaches, 10,000 trucks.

8. Maintenance of enemy occupation troops in Germany.

9. In the East all troops to withdraw behind the boundaries of August 1, 1914; fixed time not given.

10. Renunciation of the Treaties of Brest-Litovsk and Bucharest.

11. Unconditional surrender of East Africa.

12. Return of the property of the Belgian Bank, Russian and Rumanian gold.

13. Return of prisoners of war without reciprocity.

14. Surrender of 160 U-boats, 8 light cruisers, 6 dreadnoughts; the rest of the fleet to be disarmed and controlled by the Allies in neutral or Allied harbors.

15. Assurance of free transit through the Cattegat Sound; clearance of mine-fields and occupation of all forts and batteries, through which transit could be hindered.

16. The blockade remains in effect. All German ships to be captured.

17. All limitations by Germany on neutral shipping to be removed.

18. Armistice lasts thirty days.

— Reading No. 6 —

DECLARATION BY GERMAN DELEGATES ON SIGNING THE ARMISTICE [6]

When the German delegates, acting on instructions from Berlin, signed the armistice on the morning of November 11, 1918, they accepted terms which all of them regarded as shameful and unfair. Their efforts to obtain milder terms had been in vain. The four plenipotentiaries issued the following statement to indicate the reluctance with which they signed the truce.

✓   ✓   ✓

German Government will naturally endeavor with all its power to take care that the duties imposed upon it shall be carried out.

The undersigned Plenipotentiaries recognize that in certain points regard has been paid to their suggestions. They can therefore regard the comments made on November 9th on the conditions of the Armistice with Germany and the answer handed to them on November 10th as an essential condition of the whole agreement.

They must, however, allow no doubt to exist on the point that in particular the short time allowed for evacuation as well as the surrender of indispensable means of transport threaten to bring about a state of things which without its being the fault of the German Government and the German people may render impossible the further fulfilment of the conditions.

[6] Quoted in Ralph Haswell Lutz (ed.), *Fall of the German Empire, 1914-1918* (Stanford, 1932), II, 518. By permission of the Board of Trustees of Stanford University.

The undersigned Plenipotentiaries further regard it as their duty with reference to their repeated oral and written declaration once more to point out with all possible emphasis that the carrying out of this agreement must throw the German people into anarchy and famine. According to the declarations which preceded the Armistice, conditions were to be expected which while completely ensuring the military situation of our opponents would have ended the sufferings of women and children who took no part in the war.

The German people, which has held its own for fifty months against a world of enemies, will in spite of any force that may be brought to bear upon it preserve its freedom and unity.

A people of 70 millions suffers but does not die.

(*Signed*) Erzberger
Oberndorff
Winterfeldt
Vanselow

— Reading No. 7 —

ALFRED VON WEGERER DENIES GERMAN WAR GUILT[7]

Dr. Alfred von Wegerer, a German officer during the war, took the lead in combatting the thesis of German war guilt. He founded a scholarly journal, Die Kriegs-schuldfrage (The War Guilt Problem), *which he edited from 1923 to 1937 (called* Berlin Monatshefte *after 1928). As early as May 1919, Wegerer protested against the concept of German war guilt.*

✓ ✓ ✓

We cannot sign a document which our enemies call a peace. Any government which, by its signature, gives this work of the devil the halo of right, sooner or later will be driven out of office.

Is this peace a surprise to us? Unfortunately, yes. No one could possibly have believed in such cunning madness. We all expected a peace of agreement and justice. We read about it carefully and with good faith what the false prophet across the big pond promised to us and all the world. Now we can see how Old England and that revenge-laden chauvinist, Clemenceau, urged on by Foch, put together a peace like those of the old days. There is not the least trace of an understanding of the times, of any foresight into the future. There it is—a gray, bureaucrat's treaty, put together by small, narrow-minded, hate-ridden politicians. In a few years all this wicked bungling will be wiped away. . . .

[7] Alfred von Wegerer, *"Politische Zeitgedanken,"* in *Der Tag,* May 28, 1919, No. 243.

What must we do in the immediate future? We must nurture internal unity. We must hammer away at the conscience of the world through notes, protests, and communications of all kinds, until those charlatans at the head of the misled enemy nations are deposed and the field of right becomes free for setting up a true people's peace. We must begin a grand propaganda campaign. We must use film, pen, printer's ink, and brush, day and night, to achieve that goal.

But for the immediate future even all this cannot help. If the Entente invades us, then we can only stay cold-blooded, offer passive resistance whenever we can, and show them our contempt and our pride.

THE *DOLCHSTOSS* "STAB-IN-THE-BACK" THEORY, 1918 [8]

Immediately after the end of the war, German nationalists projected the Dolchstoss, *or "stab-in-the-back" theory.[9] According to this view, German arms were invincible and Germany would never have been conquered by her external enemies. The collapse was due, it was charged, to treacherous actions on the home front by radical Social Democrats and Jews in Berlin. Once again Germans sought for an explanation of weakness in the* Zerrissenheit *(dismemberment) of the German national body. A Reichstag commission investigated the problem. The first selection below gives a summary of the report by General Hermann von Kuhl. The second selection is a commentary by Albrecht Philipp, a Reichstag deputy representing the German National People's Party.*

↗   ↗   ↗

SUMMARY OF THE REPORT
BY GENERAL HERMANN VON KUHL

The expression "stab-in-the-back" (*"Dolchstoss"*) in the oft-used sense, as if the country had attacked the victori-

[8] Germany, Reichstag, *Untersuchungsausschuss über die Weltkriegsverantwortlichkeit. Vierter Unterausschuss, Die Ursachen des deutschen Zusammenbruches im Jahre 1918. Vierte Reihe im Werk des Untersuchungsausschusses,* Deutsche Verlagsgesellschaft für Politik und Geschichte m. b. H. (Berlin, 12 vol. in 15, 1925-1929), VI, 39.
    The second excerpt is from *ibid., IV,* 15.

[9] This term was first used in a report from England to the *Neue Züricher Zeitung* of December 1, 1918: "As far as the German army is concerned, the general view is summarized in these words: It was stabbed in the back by the civil population."

ous army in the rear and as if the war had been lost for this reason alone, is not accurate. We succumbed for many reasons.

It is certain, however, that a pacifistic, international, anti-military, and revolutionary undermining of the army took place which contributed in no small measure to the harm done and the disintegration of the army. It originated at home, but the blame does not attach to the entire population, which in the four and a half years of war endured superhuman sufferings; it attaches only to the agitators and corrupters of the people and of the army who for political reasons strove to poison the bravely-fighting forces.

The effects of this pernicious activity became especially apparent when, after the failure of our offensive in the summer of 1918, the war seemed hopelessly lost. But the subversive work had long before been systematically begun. One should therefore speak, not of a stab in the back, but of a *poisoning of the army*.

The expression "stab-in-the-back" may, however, be applied to the sudden and devastating effects of the *revolution* itself. It literally attacked the army from the rear, disorganized the lines of communication, prevented the forwarding of supplies, and destroyed all order and discipline as if at a blow. It made all further fighting impossible and compelled the acceptance of any armistice terms. The revolution was not the result of the collapse of the offensive, although this substantially furthered its outbreak and its effects. On the contrary, the revolution was prepared long beforehand.

The revolution further gave rise to the danger of the complete dissolution of the army during the retreat and thus of a monstrous catastrophe. This danger was averted only with the greatest difficulty.

↗   ↗   ↗

THE STATEMENT OF CHAIRMAN ALBRECHT PHILIPP
ON KUHL'S REPORT

In view of the many interpretations of the expression "stab-in-the-back," it is better not to use this term for the influences which, coming from home, weakened the army's will to fight. That such influences were present in large number cannot be denied. Heavy blame doubtless lies with those circles which fostered the efforts to disintegrate or poison the armed forces. But the available factual material does not suffice to prove that these circles alone were to blame. Von Kuhl declares quite correctly: "We succumbed for many reasons." All those revolutionary efforts can be blamed, not for the circumstance that we had to evacuate the West and thus give up the prospects of winning the war, but for the way in which the end of the war overwhelmed Germany. The expression "stab-in-the-back" is absolutely correct as a criticism of the revolution as a single event, but it can be applied only with limitations to the motive powers of the development which prepared the ground for the German Revolution.

THE ABDICATION OF WILLIAM II, NOVEMBER 28, 1918 [10]

On November 10, 1918, when it became obvious that World War I was irretrievably lost, William II, Supreme War Lord, fled across the German border to Holland. Two weeks later, William, creator of Germany's New Course, father of her Big Navy, fanatical proponent of "the good old Prussian spirit," issued this abdication proclamation.

↗   ↗   ↗

I herewith renounce for all time claims to the Throne of Prussia and to the German Imperial Throne connected therewith. At the same time I release all officials of the German Empire and of Prussia, as well as all officers, non-commissioned officers and men of the Navy and of the Prussian Army, as well as the troops of the federated states of Germany, from the oath of fidelity which they tendered to me as their Emperor, King, and Commander-in-Chief. I expect of them that until the re-establishment of order in the German Empire they shall render assistance to those in actual power in Germany, in protecting the German people from the threatening dangers of anarchy, famine, and foreign rule.

Proclaimed under our own hand and with the Imperial Seal attached.

Amerongen, 28 November, 1918

[*Signed*] WILLIAM

[10] F. Purlitz, *Die deutsche Revolution* (Berlin, n.d.), I, 32.

— Reading No. 10 —

THE SPARTACIST MANIFESTO, NOVEMBER 29, 1918 [11]

The establishment of the German Republic was complicated by the existence of a revolutionary movement, inspired by Bolshevism, which became known as "Spartacist," after the pseudonym of its leader, Karl Liebknecht. As Communists, the Spartacists were as much opposed to a liberal or Socialist republic as they had been to the old imperial Germany. They proclaimed "the dictatorship of the proletariat" and established councils in imitation of the soviets in Russia. The following manifesto, which expressed the Spartacist position, was composed by Klara Zetkin, Franz Mehring, Rosa Luxemburg, and Karl Liebknecht.

✓   ✓   ✓

PROLETARIANS! MEN AND WOMEN OF LABOR! COMRADES!

The revolution has made its entry into Germany. The masses of the soldiers, who for four years were driven to the slaughterhouse for the sake of capitalistic profits, the masses of workers, who for four years were exploited, crushed, and starved, have revolted. That fearful tool of oppression—Prussian militarism, that scourge of humanity —lies broken on the ground. Its most noticeable representatives, and therewith the most noticeable of those guilty of this war, the Kaiser and the Crown Prince, have

[11] *Die Rote Fahne* (organ of the Spartacus party), Berlin, November 26, 1918; quoted in *The New York Times*, November 29, 1918.

fled from the country. Workers' and Soldiers' Councils have been formed everywhere.

Proletarians of all countries, we do not say that in Germany all the power has really been lodged in the hands of the working people, that the complete triumph of the proletarian revolution has already been attained. There still sit in the government all those Socialists who in August, 1914, abandoned our most precious possession, the International, who for four years betrayed the German working class and at the same time the International.

But, proletarians of all countries, now the German proletarian himself is speaking to you. We believe we have the right to appeal before your forum in his name. From the first day of this war we endeavored to do our international duty by fighting that criminal government with all our power, and branding it as the one really guilty of the war.

Now, at this moment, we are justified before history, before the International, and before the German proletariat. The masses agree with us enthusiastically; constantly widening circles of the proletariat share the knowledge that the hour has struck for a settlement with capitalist class rule. . . .

The imperialism of all countries knows no "understanding"; it knows only one right—capital's profits; it knows only one language—the sword; it knows only one method —violence. And if it is now talking in all countries, in yours as well as ours, about the "League of Nations," "disarmament," "rights of small nations," "self-determination of the peoples," it is merely using the customary lying phrases of the rulers for the purpose of lulling to sleep the watchfulness of the proletariat.

Proletarians of all countries! This must be the last war! We owe that to the twelve million murdered victims; we owe that to our children; we owe that to humanity. . . .

We call to you: "Arise for the struggle! Arise for action! The time for empty manifestoes, platonic resolutions, and high-sounding words has gone by! The hour of action has struck for the International!" We ask you to elect Workers' and Soldiers' Councils everywhere that will seize political power and, together with us, will restore peace.

Not Lloyd George and Poincaré, not Sonnino, Wilson, and Erzberger or Scheidemann; these must not be allowed to make peace. Peace is to be concluded under the waving banner of the socialist world revolution.

Proletarians of all countries! We call upon you to complete the work of socialist liberation, to give a human aspect to the disfigured world, and to make true those words with which we often greeted each other in the old days and which we sang as we parted: "And the International shall be the human race."

— Reading No. 11 —

JOINT ANNOUNCEMENT OF THE INDEPENDENTS AND THE COMMUNISTS, JANUARY 5, 1919 [12]

When Ebert tried to dismiss Emil Eichhorn, the chief of Berlin's police, the Independent Socialists and the Communists issued a joint manifesto calling for a "mighty demonstration" against the government. The response to this summons was so great that the Ebert government was forced to fight for its life.

✓   ✓   ✓

Workers! Comrades! The Ebert government with its accomplices in the Prussian ministry is seeking to uphold its power with the bayonet, and to secure for itself the favor of the capitalist bourgeoisie whose interests it has always secretly supported. The blow that has fallen upon the chief of the Berlin police was in reality aimed at the whole German proletariat, at the whole German revolution. Workers! Comrades! That cannot, must not, be tolerated! Up, therefore, to a mighty demonstration! Show the oppressors your power today, prove to them that the revolutionary spirit of the November days is not yet dead in you! Meet today . . . to stage a great mass demonstration! Come in your thousands! Your freedom, your future, the fate of the revolution, are at stake. Down with the tyranny of Ebert and Scheidemann. . . . Long live revolutionary international socialism!

[12] Quoted in S. William Halperin, *Germany Tried Democracy* (New York, 1965), p. 120. (Norton Library edition.) By permission of Thomas Y. Crowell Company.

— Reading No. 12 —

THE MILITARY MACHINE REVIVED: BERLIN IN MID-JANUARY, 1919 [13]

A correspondent for the Manchester Guardian *described the situation in Berlin in mid-January 1919 in the following terms. Later events proved his prophecies to be true.*

✓   ✓   ✓

The formidable military machine, which seemed to be crushed forever, has risen again with astounding rapidity. Prussian officers are stalking the streets of Berlin, soldiers marching, shouting and shooting at their command. Indeed Ebert and Scheidemann very likely got more than they bargained for. Already there are signs that the newly-risen military system is disposed to take the law into its own hands and it remains to be seen how long it will be content to remain the instrument of the present government. The coalition between Government, Socialists, the middle classes, Pan-Germans, and militarists is for the moment perfect, and Germany is now under the control of the same elements which applauded and carried on the war. They have crushed, or are in a fair way of crushing, the political sections which combatted the German war party for years. It is a fact which will scarcely fail to affect Germany's international position at the present juncture. At the same time there is no reason at all to believe that the Government's military victory will make for internal peace, order and stability. Everything points to the contrary.

[13] *Manchester Guardian,* January 15, 1919.

— Reading No. 13 —

GUSTAV LANDAUER ON THE LOST REVOLUTION, JANUARY 21, 1919 [14]

Some observers believed that the failure of the German Revolution of 1918-1919 was due to the fact that it was impossible to bring about a change to democracy in a country where the reactionary mentality was so deeply engraved in the minds of the citizens. Gustav Landauer, a Bavarian Socialist, commented on this view.

✦　　　✦　　　✦

Only a few people rejected the German war from the beginning and saw that it was what its promoters had designed it to be from the beginning: a German war. The conflict had military, political, and economic results, among which was the fact that a not insignificant number of workers and women were stimulated to a revolutionary mood. A few determined individuals supported the revolution with fierce energy, in the belief that they bore the future—socialism—within themselves. They wanted to be creative, not merely tolerate things as they were. Those who helped them were but a small minority; all others need a long and intensive education in truly democratic institutions. Of this minority many were lost to the revolution the day after it took place. Before the revolution they were soldiers plagued beyond endurance; in the revolution they were death-defying rebels; on the day of triumph they were soldiers who had won salvation; the next day they were fearful and anxious *Bürger*.

[14] *Die Republik,* January 21, 1919.

— Reading No. 14 —

THE TREATY OF VERSAILLES IS PRESENTED TO THE GERMANS, MAY 7, 1919 [15]

After the completion of the peace treaty, the German delegates were summoned to Versailles to accept it on behalf of their government. They had taken no part in the proceedings thus far and had no idea of what the treaty contained. They were told that they would not be permitted to discuss it. The dramatic scene was described by Thomas A. Bailey in this passage.

✓ ✓ ✓

The Treaty of Versailles was formally presented to the German representatives on May 7, 1919, by coincidence the fourth anniversary of the sinking of the *Lusitania.*

The scene was the Trianon Palace at Versailles. The day was one of surpassing loveliness, and brilliant spring sunlight flooded the room. Dr. Walter Simons, Commissioner-General of the German delegation, noted that "outside of the big window at my right there was a wonderful cherry tree in bloom, and it seemed to me the only reality when compared with the performance in the hall. This cherry tree and its kind will still be blooming when the states whose representatives gathered here exist no longer."

[15] Thomas A. Bailey, in *Wilson and the Peace-Makers* (New York, 1947), pp. 288-290. By permission of The Macmillan Company.

The crowd was small, for the room was small—merely the delegates of both sides, with their assistants, and a few carefully selected press representatives. The grim-visaged Clemenceau sat at the center of the main table: Wilson at his right, Lloyd George at his left.

The air was surcharged with electricity: German and Allied diplomats had not met face to face since the fateful summer of 1914. Would the Germans do something to offend the proprieties?

When all were seated, the doors swung open. At the cry, *"Messieurs les plénipotentiaires allemands!"* the whole assembly rose and stood in silence while the German delegates filed in before their conquerors and sat at a table facing Clemenceau.

The Tiger rose to his feet, and, his voice vibrant with the venom of 1871, almost spat out his speech with staccato precision: "It is neither the time nor the place for superfluous words. . . . The time has come when we must settle our accounts. You have asked for peace. We are ready to give you peace."

Already a secretary had quietly walked over to the table at which the Germans sat, and laid before them the thick, two-hundred-odd-page treaty—"the book."

With Clemenceau still standing, the pale, black-clad Count Brockdorff-Rantzau, head of the German delegation, began reading his reply—*seated*.

An almost perceptible gasp swept the room, for the failure of the German to rise was taken as a studied discourtesy. Some felt that he was too nervous and shaken to stand. Others felt that he wanted to snub his "conquerors." The truth is that he planned to sit, not wishing to stand like a culprit before a judge to receive sentence.

Nothing could better reflect the spirit of the Germans. They felt that the war had been more or less a stalemate; they had laid down their arms expecting to negotiate with a chivalrous foe. As equals, why should they rise like criminals before the Allied bar?

If Brockdorff-Rantzau's posture was unfortunate, his words and the intonation of his words were doubly so.

The Germans had not yet read the Treaty, but they had every reason to believe that it would be severe. They had not been allowed to participate in its negotiation;

they would not be allowed to discuss its provisions *orally* with their conquerors. Brockdorff-Rantzau decided to make the most of this his only opportunity to meet his adversaries face to face and comment on the unread Treaty. Both his manner and his words were sullen, arrogant, unrepentant.

Speaking with great deliberation and without the usual courteous salutation to the presiding officer, he began by saying that the Germans were under "no illusions" as to the extent of their defeat and the degree of their "powerlessness." This was not true, for both he and his people were under great illusions.

Then he referred defiantly but inaccurately to the demand that the Germans acknowledge that "we alone are guilty of having caused the war. Such a confession in my mouth would be a lie." And the word "lie" fairly hissed from between his teeth.

Bitterly he mentioned the "hundreds of thousands" of German non-combatants who had perished since Armistice Day as a result of Allied insistence on continuing the blockade during the peace negotiations. This shaft struck home, especially to the heart of Lloyd George.

When the echo of Brockdorff-Rantzau's last tactless word had died away, Clemenceau spoke. His face had gone red during the harangue, but he had held himself in check with remarkable self-restraint. Harshly and peremptorily he steam-rolled the proceedings to an end: "Has anybody any more observations to offer? Does no one wish to speak? If not, the meeting is closed."

The German delegates marched out, facing a battery of clicking moving picture cameras. Brockdorf-Rantzau lighted a cigarette with trembling fingers.

Lloyd George, who had snapped an ivory paper knife in his hands, remarked angrily: "It is hard to have won the war and to have to listen to that."

Thus, within a half-hour, was compressed one of the greatest dramas of all time.

— Reading No. 15 —

THE GERMAN GOVERNMENT ACCEPTS THE PEACE TREATY, JUNE 23, 1919 [16]

The German government was required by ultimatum to accept the Allied terms of peace no later than six P.M. on June 23, 1919. Two hours before the expiration of the ultimatum, the following note was sent from Berlin to Versailles.

✦ ✦ ✦

The government of the German republic is overwhelmed to learn from the last communication of the Allied and Associated Powers that the Allies are resolved to enforce, with all the power at their command, the acceptance even of those provisions in the treaty which, without having any material significance, are designed to deprive the German people of their honor. The honor of the German people cannot be injured by an act of violence. The German people, after their terrible sufferings during these last years, are wholly without the means of defending their honor against the outside world. Yielding to overpowering might, the government of the German republic declares itself ready to accept and sign the peace treaty imposed by the Allied and Associated governments. But in so doing, the government of the German republic in no wise abandons its conviction that these conditions of peace represent injustice without example.

[16] Quoted in S. William Halperin, *Germany Tried Democracy* (New York, 1965), p. 152. (Norton Library edition.) By permission of Thomas Y. Crowell Company.

— Reading No. 16 —

THE TREATY OF VERSAILLES, JUNE 28, 1919 [17]

The Treaty of Versailles comprised fifteen parts, including 144 articles and nearly a score of annexes. The extracts below, from Part V, contain the military, naval, and air clauses, which were designed to disarm Germany and prevent her from waging future wars. These clauses were violated in one way or another from the very beginning. The territorial clauses could not be changed without further warfare, which Hitler attempted in 1939. Clauses on the Rhineland forbade Germany "to maintain or construct any fortifications either on the left bank of the Rhine or on the right bank to the west of a line drawn fifty kilometers to the east of the Rhine" (Article 42), and provided for Allied occupation of the German territory to the west of the Rhine for fifteen years (Article 428).

✓   ✓   ✓

PART V

In order to render possible the initiation of a general limitation of the armaments of all nations, Germany undertakes strictly to observe the military, naval and air clauses which follow.

[17] Great Britain, *Parliamentary Papers 1919. Treaty of Peace between the Allied and Associated Powers and Germany,* signed at Versailles, 28th of June, 1919, Vol. LIII, cmd. 153.

Section I: Military Clauses

Chapter I: Effectives and Cadres of the German Army

ARTICLE 159. The German military forces shall be demobilized and reduced as prescribed hereinafter.

ARTICLE 160. (1) By a date which must be not later than March 31, 1920, the German Army must not comprise more than seven divisions of infantry and three divisions of cavalry.

After that date the total number of effectives in the Army of the States constituting Germany must not exceed one hundred thousand men, including officers and establishments of depots. The Army shall be devoted exclusively to the maintenance of order within the territory and to the control of the frontiers.

The total effective strength of officers, including the personnel of staffs, whatever their composition, must not exceed four thousand.

(2) Divisions and Army Corps headquarters staffs shall be organised in accordance with Table No. 1 annexed to this Section.

The number and strengths of the units of infantry, artillery, engineers, technical services and troops laid down in the aforesaid Table constitute maxima which must not be exceeded.

The following units may each have their own depot:

An Infantry regiment;
A Cavalry regiment;
A regiment of Field Artillery;
A battalion of Pioneers.

(3) The divisions must not be grouped under more than two army corps headquarters staffs.

The maintenance of formation of forces differently grouped or of other organisations for the command of troops or for preparation for war is forbidden.

The Great German General Staff and all similar organisations shall be dissolved and may not be reconstituted in any form. . . .

CHAPTER II: ARMAMENT, MUNITIONS AND MATERIAL

ARTICLE 168. The manufacture of arms, munitions, or any war material, shall only be carried out in factories or works the location of which shall be communicated to and approved by the Governments of the Principal Allied and Associated Powers, and the number of which they retain the right to restrict.

Within three months from the coming into force of the present Treaty, all other establishments for the manufacture, preparation, storage or design of arms, munitions, or any war material whatever shall be closed down. The same applies to all arsenals except those used as depots for the authorised stocks of munitions. Within the same period the personnel of these arsenals will be dismissed. . . .

ARTICLE 170. Importation into Germany of arms, munitions and war material of every kind shall be strictly prohibited.

The same applies to the manufacture for, and export to, foreign countries of arms, munitions and war material of every kind.

ARTICLE 171. The use of asphyxiating, poisonous or other gases and all analogous liquids, materials or devices being prohibited, their manufacture and importation are strictly forbidden in Germany.

The same applies to materials specially intended for the manufacture, storage and use of the said products or devices.

The manufacture and the importation into Germany of armoured cars, tanks and all similar constructions suitable for use in war are also prohibited. . . .

SECTION II: NAVAL CLAUSES

ARTICLE 181. After the expiration of a period of two months from the coming into force of the present Treaty the German naval forces in commission must not exceed:

6 battleships of the *Deutschland* or *Lothringen* type,
6 light cruisers,
12 destroyers,
12 torpedo boats,

or an equal number of ships constructed to replace
them. . . .

No submarines are to be included.

All other warships, except where there is provision to
the contrary in the present Treaty, must be placed in
reserve or devoted to commercial purposes. . . .

ARTICLE 183.   After the expiration of a period of two
months from the coming into force of the present Treaty
the total personnel of the German Navy, including the
manning of the fleet, coast defences, signal stations, administration and other land services, must not exceed
fifteen thousand, including officers and men of all grades
and corps.

The total strength of officers and warrant officers must
not exceed fifteen hundred.

Within two months from the coming into force of the
present Treaty the personnel in excess of the above
strength shall be demobilised.

No naval or military corps or reserve force in connection with the Navy may be organised in Germany without being included in the above strength. . . .

ARTICLE 191.   The construction or acquisition of any
submarine, even for commercial purposes, shall be forbidden in Germany.

SECTION III: AIR CLAUSES

ARTICLE 198.   The armed forces of Germany must
not include any military or naval air forces.

Germany may, during a period not extending beyond
October 1, 1919, maintain a maximum number of one
hundred seaplanes or flying boats, which shall be exclusively employed in searching for submarine mines,
shall be furnished with the necessary equipment for this
purpose, and shall in no case carry arms, munitions or
bombs of any nature whatever.

In addition to the engines installed in the seaplanes or
flying boats above mentioned, one spare engine may be
provided for each engine of each of these craft.

No dirigible shall be kept. . . .

SECTION IV: INTER-ALLIED COMMISSIONS OF CONTROL

ARTICLE 203. All the military, naval and air clauses contained in the present Treaty, for the execution of which a time-limit is prescribed, shall be executed by Germany under the control of Inter-Allied Commissions specially appointed for this purpose by the Principal Allied and Associated Powers.

ARTICLE 204. The Inter-Allied Commissions of Control will be specially charged with the duty of seeing to the complete execution of the delivery, destruction, demolition and rendering things useless to be carried out at the expense of the German Government in accordance with the present Treaty.

They will communicate to the German authorities the decisions which the Principal Allied and Associated Powers have reserved the right to take, or which the execution of the military, naval and air clauses may necessitate. . . .

— Reading No. 17 —

A PAN-GERMAN NEWSPAPER CALLS FOR VENGEANCE, JUNE 28, 1919 [18]

On June 28, 1919, a Pan-German newspaper, the Deutsche Zeitung, *appeared with a black mourning band surrounding the following statement on its front page.*

✓　　　✓　　　✓

Vengeance! German nation! Today in the Hall of Mirrors at Versailles a disgraceful treaty is being signed. Never forget it! On that spot where, in the glorious year of 1871, the German Empire in all its glory began, today German honor is dragged to the grave. Never forget it! The German people, with unceasing labor, will push forward to reconquer that place among the nations of the world to which they are entitled. There will be vengeance for the shame of 1919.

[18] *Deutsche Zeitung,* June 28, 1919.

— Reading No. 18 —

THE WEIMAR CONSTITUTION [19]

*In February 1919 the National Constituent Assembly
was convened at Weimar, a small town on the river
Elbe. A constitution guaranteeing federal rights, and
providing for a bicameral legislative body, a seven-year
presidential office, and proportional representation in voting was adopted on July 31, 1919, and signed on August
11, 1919. Extracts from the Weimar Constitution are re-
printed here.*

✓   ✓   ✓

Preamble:

The German people, united in all their elements, and
inspired by the will to renew and strengthen their Reich
in liberty and justice, to preserve peace at home and
abroad and to foster social progress, have established the
following Constitution:

CHAPTER I: STRUCTURE AND FUNCTIONS OF
THE REICH

SECTION I: REICH AND STATES

ARTICLE 1.   The German Reich is a Republic. Political
authority emanates from the people.

   ARTICLE 2:   The territory of the Reich consists of the
territories of the German member states. . . .

   ARTICLE 3.   The Reich colors are black, red, and gold.
The merchant flag is black, white, and red, with the
Reich colors in the upper inside corner.

[19] Translated from *Die Verfassung des Deutschen Reiches vom
11. August 1919,* the official text of the 7th edition
(Leipzig, 1930).

ARTICLE 4.   The generally accepted rules of international law are to be considered as binding integral parts of the German Reich.

ARTICLE 5.   Political authority is exercised in national affairs by the national government in accordance with the Constitution of the Reich, and in state affairs by the state governments in accordance with state constitutions. . . .

ARTICLE 12.   Insofar as the Reich does not exercise its jurisdiction, such jurisdiction remains with the states . . . with the exception of cases in which the Reich possesses exclusive jurisdiction. . . .

ARTICLE 17.   Every state must have a republican constitution. The representatives of the people must be elected by universal, equal, direct, and secret suffrage of all German citizens, both men and women, in accordance with the principles of proportional representation.

SECTION II: THE REICHSTAG

ARTICLE 20.   The Reichstag is composed of the delegates of the German people.

ARTICLE 21.   The delegates are representatives of the whole people. They are subject only to their own conscience and are not bound by any instructions.

ARTICLE 22.   The delegates are elected by universal, equal, direct, and secret suffrage by men and women over twenty years of age, according to the principle of proportional representation. Election day must be a Sunday or a public holiday.

ARTICLE 23.   The Reichstag is elected for four years. New elections must take place at the latest on the sixtieth day after this term has run its course. . . .

ARTICLE 32.   For decisions of the Reichstag a simple majority vote is necessary, unless the Constitution prescribes another proportion of votes. . . .

ARTICLE 33.   The Reichstag and its committees may require the presence of the Reich Chancellor and every Reich Minister. . . .

SECTION III: THE REICH PRESIDENT AND THE REICH CABINET

ARTICLE 41.   The Reich President is elected by the

whole German people. Every German who has completed his thirty-fifth year is eligible for election. . . .

ARTICLE 42. On assuming office, the Reich President shall take the following oath before the Reichstag:

> I swear to devote my energies to the well-being of the German people, to further their interests, to guard them from injury, to maintain the Constitution and the laws of the Reich, to fulfill my duties conscientiously, and to administer justice for all.

It is permissible to add a religious affirmation.

ARTICLE 43. The term of office of the Reich President is seven years. Re-election is permissible.

Before the expiration of his term, the Reich President, upon motion of the Reichstag, may be recalled by a popular vote. The decision of the Reichstag shall be by a two-thirds majority. Through such decision the Reich President is denied any further exercise of his office. The rejection of the recall motion by the popular referendum counts as a new election and results in the dissolution of the Reichstag. . . .

ARTICLE 48. If any state does not fulfill the duties imposed upon it by the Constitution or the laws of the Reich, the Reich President may enforce such duties with the aid of the armed forces.

In the event that the public order and security are seriously disturbed or endangered, the Reich President may take the measures necessary for their restoration, intervening, if necessary, with the aid of the armed forces. For this purpose he may abrogate temporarily, wholly or in part, the fundamental principles laid down in Articles 114, 115, 117, 118, 123, 124, and 153.

The Reich President must, without delay, inform the Reichstag of all measures taken under Paragraph 1 or Paragraph 2 of this Article. These measures may be rescinded on demand of the Reichstag. . . .

ARTICLE 50. All orders and decrees of the Reich President, including those relating to the armed forces, in order to be valid, must be countersigned by the Reich Chancellor or by the appropriate Reich Minister. Responsibility is assumed through the countersignature. . . .

ARTICLE 52.   The Reich Cabinet consists of the Reich Chancellor and the Reich Ministers.

ARTICLE 53.   The Reich Chancellor and, on his recommendation, the Reich Ministers, are appointed and dismissed by the Reich President.

ARTICLE 54.   The Reich Chancellor and the Reich Ministers require for the exercise of their office the confidence of the Reichstag. Any one of them must resign if the Reichstag by formal resolution withdraws its confidence.

ARTICLE 55.   The Reich Chancellor presides over the government of the Reich and conducts its affairs according to the rules of procedure laid down by the government of the Reich and approved by the Reich President.

ARTICLE 56.   The Reich Chancellor determines the political program of the Reich and assumes responsibility to the Reichstag. Within this general policy each Reich Minister conducts independently the office entrusted to him and is held individually responsible to the Reichstag.

SECTION IV: THE REICHSRAT

ARTICLE 60.   A Reichsrat is formed to give the German states representation in the law-making and administration of the Reich.

ARTICLE 61.   Each state has at least one vote in the Reichsrat. In the case of the larger states one vote shall be assigned for every million inhabitants.[20] . . . No single state shall have more than two-fifths of the total number of votes. . . .

ARTICLE 63.   The states shall be represented in the Reichsrat by members of their governments. . . .

SECTION V: REICH LEGISLATION

ARTICLE 68.   Bills are introduced by the Reich cabinet, with the concurrence of the Reichsrat, or by members of the Reichstag. Reich laws shall be enacted by the Reichstag. . . .

ARTICLE 73.   A law of the Reichstag must be submitted to popular referendum before its proclamation, if the Reich President, within one month of its passage, so decides. . . .

[20] Amended by law of March 24, 1921, to "every 700,000 inhabitants."

ARTICLE 74. The Reichsrat may protest against laws passed by the Reichstag. In case of such protest, the law is returned to the Reichstag, which may override the objection by a two-thirds majority. The Reich President must either promulgate the law within three months or call for a referendum. . . .

ARTICLE 76. The Constitution may be amended by law, but acts . . . amending the Constitution can only take effect if two-thirds of the legal number of members are present and at least two-thirds of those present consent. . . .

SECTION VI: THE REICH ADMINISTRATION

[*Articles 78-101 cover the jurisdiction of the Reich Administration in such matters as foreign affairs, national defense, colonial policies, customs, national budgets, postal and telegraph services, railroads, and waterways.*]

SECTION VII: ADMINISTRATION OF JUSTICE

[*Articles 102-108 provide for a hierarchy of Reich and state courts, with judges appointed by the Reich President for life.*]

CHAPTER II: FUNDAMENTAL RIGHTS AND DUTIES OF THE GERMANS

SECTION I: THE INDIVIDUAL

ARTICLE 109. All Germans are equal before the law. Men and women have the same fundamental civil rights and duties. Public legal privileges or disadvantages of birth or of rank are abolished. Titles of nobility . . . may be bestowed no longer. . . . Orders and decorations shall not be conferred by the state. No German shall accept titles or orders from a foreign government.

ARTICLE 110. Citizenship of the Reich and the states is acquired in accordance with the provisions of a Reich law. . . .

ARTICLE 111. All Germans shall enjoy liberty of travel and residence throughout the whole Reich. . . .

ARTICLE 112. Every German is permitted to emigrate to a foreign country. . . .

ARTICLE 114. Personal liberty is inviolable. Curtailment or deprivation of personal liberty by a public authority is permissible only by authority of law.

Persons who have been deprived of their liberty must be informed at the latest on the following day by whose authority and for what reasons they have been held. They shall receive the opportunity without delay of submitting objections to their deprivation of liberty.

ARTICLE 115. The house of every German is his sanctuary and is inviolable. Exceptions are permitted only by authority of law. . . .

ARTICLE 117. The secrecy of letters and all postal, telegraph, and telephone communications is inviolable. Exceptions are inadmissible except by national law.

ARTICLE 118. Every German has the right, within the limits of the general laws, to express his opinion freely by word, in writing, in print, in picture form, or in any other way. . . . Censorship is forbidden. . . .

SECTION II: THE GENERAL WELFARE

ARTICLE 123. All Germans have the right to assemble peacefully and unarmed without giving notice and without special permission. . . .

ARTICLE 124. All Germans have the right to form associations and societies for purposes not contrary to the criminal law. . . .

ARTICLE 126. Every German has the right to petition. . . .

SECTION III: RELIGION AND RELIGIOUS SOCIETIES

ARTICLE 135. All inhabitants of the Reich enjoy full religious freedom and freedom of conscience. The free exercise of religion is guaranteed by the Constitution and is under public protection. . . .

ARTICLE 137. There is no state church. . . .

SECTION IV: EDUCATION AND THE SCHOOLS

ARTICLE 142. Art, science, and the teaching thereof are free. . . .

ARTICLE 143. The education of the young is to be provided for by means of public institutions. . . .

ARTICLE 144. The entire school system is under the supervision of the state. . . .

Article 145. Attendance at school is compulsory. . . .

Section V: ECONOMIC LIFE

Article 151. The regulation of economic life must be compatible with the principles of justice, with the aim of attaining humane conditions of existence for all. Within these limits the economic liberty of the individual is assured. . . .

Article 152. Freedom of contract prevails . . . in accordance with the laws. . . .

Article 153. The right of private property is guaranteed by the Constitution. . . . Expropriation of property may take place . . . by due process of law. . . .

Article 159. Freedom of association for the preservation and promotion of labor and economic conditions is guaranteed to everyone and to all vocations. All agreements and measures attempting to restrict or restrain this freedom are unlawful. . . .

Article 161. The Reich shall organize a comprehensive system of [social] insurance. . . .

Article 165. Workers and employees are called upon to cooperate, on an equal footing, with employers in the regulation of wages and of the conditions of labor, as well as in the general development of the productive forces. . . .

CONCLUDING PROVISIONS

Article 181. . . . The German people have passed and adopted this Constitution through their National Assembly. It comes into force with the date of its proclamation.

Schwarzburg, August 11, 1919.

The Reich President
EBERT
The Reich Cabinet
BAUER
ERZBERGER   HERMANN MÜLLER   DR. DAVID
NOSKE   SCHMIDT
SCHLICKE   GIESBERTS   DR. BAYER
DR. BELL

— Reading No. 19 —

THE KAPP *PUTSCH*: A SELF-PROCLAIMED "REICH CHANCELLOR" ADDRESSES THE GERMAN PEOPLE, MARCH 13, 1920 [21]

On the morning of March 13, 1920, after a coup d'état supported by a dissident naval brigade, Dr. Wolfgang Kapp, representative of a rightist conspiracy, proclaimed himself chancellor. His first manifesto to the German people called for a government of order, freedom, and action. It will be noted from the following condensed excerpts that Kapp tried to curry favor with the workers by promising them far-reaching concessions.

↑   ↑   ↑

The National Assembly has defied the constitution by postponing the elections to the fall. Instead of obeying the constitution, which it solemnly enacted, the ruling party has already deprived the people of the right to elect their president.

The hour to rescue Germany has been lost. There remains only a government of action.

What are our tasks?

The government will fulfill its obligations under the peace treaty, in so far as it does not violate the honor and the life of the German people. . . .

[21] Quoted in Johannes Hohlfeld, *Die Weimarer Republik, 1919-1933* (Berlin and Munich, n.d.), III, 113-114. Courtesy of Giersch & Co. Translated by the editor.

The government stands for economic freedom. . . .

The government will ruthlessly suppress strikes and sabotage. Strikes mean treason to the people, the Fatherland, and the future.

This will not be a government of one-sided capitalism, but it will defend German labor against the harsh fate of international slavery under finance capitalism. . . .

The government regards it as its most holy duty to protect the war wounded and widows of our fallen fighters. . . .

The government promises freedom of religion. . . .

We shall govern not with theories but through the practical needs of the state and the people. The government will be an objective judge in the current battle between capital and labor. We decline to favor any party, whether Right or Left. We recognize only German citizens. . . .

Every person must do his duty! Today work is the most important duty for any person. Germany must be a moral working community.

The colors of the German Republic are black-white-red!

The Reich Chancellor
KAPP

— Reading No. 20 —

THE TWENTY-FIVE POINTS OF THE GERMAN WORKERS' PARTY, FEBRUARY 25, 1920 [22]

On September 19, 1919, Adolf Hitler, disgruntled war veteran and fanatical nationalist, joined a small, obscure political group in Munich called "The German Workers' Party," a remnant of the once-powerful Pan-Germanic Fatherland Party. The first public meeting of this new organization was held at a Munich beer hall on February 24, 1920. Although Hitler was not the party leader at this time, he delivered a speech in which he demanded that the program drawn up by leaders of the group be adopted. The program was the work of Anton Drexler, a bespectacled toolmaker who had originated the idea of founding a nationalist-minded workers' party; Gottfried Eckart, a journalist and editor of the Völkischer Beobachter, which was later to become the official Nazi party newspaper; and Hitler, who later wrote: "When I finally closed the meeting, we were not alone in feeling that a wolf had been born which was destined to break into the herd of swindlers and misleaders of the people."

✦   ✦   ✦

The program of the German Workers' Party is limited as to period. The leaders have no intention, once the

---

[22] Raymond E. Murphy (ed.), *National Socialism*, U.S. Department of State, Publication 1864 (Washington, 1943), pp. 222-225. It was not until August 1920 that the name of The German Workers' Party was changed to The National Socialist German Workers' Party (National-sozialistische Deutsche Arbeiterpartei—N.S.D.A.P., or Nazi party).

aims announced in it have been achieved, of setting up fresh ones, merely in order to increase the discontent of the masses artificially, and so ensure the continued existence of the party.

1. We demand the union of all Germans to form a Great Germany on the basis of the right of self-determination enjoyed by nations.

2. We demand equality of rights for the German people in its dealings with other nations, and abolition of the peace treaties of Versailles and Saint-Germain.

3. We demand land and territory (colonies) for the nourishment of our people and for settling our excess population.

4. None but members of the nation may be citizens of the state. None but those of German blood, whatever their creed, may be members of the nation. No Jew, therefore, may be a member of the nation.

5. Anyone who is not a citizen of the state may live in Germany only as a guest and must be regarded as being subject to foreign laws.

6. The right of voting on the leadership and legislation is to be enjoyed by the state alone. We demand therefore that all official appointments, of whatever kind, whether in the Reich, in the country, or in the smaller localities, shall be granted to citizens of the state alone. We oppose the corrupting custom of Parliament of filling posts merely with a view to party considerations, and without reference to character or capacity.

7. We demand that the state shall make it its first duty to promote the industry and livelihood of citizens of the state. If it is not possible to nourish the entire population of the state, foreign nationals (non-citizens of the state) must be excluded from the Reich.

8. All non-German immigration must be prevented. . . .

9. All citizens of the state shall be equal as regards rights and duties.

10. It must be the first duty of each citizen of the state to work with his mind or with his body. The activities of the individual may not clash with the interests of the whole, but must proceed within the frame of the community and be for the general good.

We demand therefore:

11.   Abolition of incomes unearned by work.

12.   In view of the enormous sacrifice of life and property demanded of a nation by every war, personal enrichment due to a war must be regarded as a crime against the nation. We demand therefore ruthless confiscation of all war gains.

13.   We demand nationalization of all businesses (trusts). . . .

14.   We demand that the profits from wholesale trade shall be shared.

15.   We demand extensive development of provision for old age.

16.   We demand creation and maintenance of a healthy middle class, immediate communalization of wholesale business premises, and their lease at a cheap rate to small traders, and that extreme consideration shall be shown to all small purveyors to the state, district authorities, and smaller localities.

17.   We demand land reform suitable to our national requirements. . . .

18.   We demand ruthless prosecution of those whose activities are injurious to the common interest. Sordid criminals against the nation, usurers, profiteers, etc., must be punished with death, whatever their creed or race.

19.   We demand that the Roman Law, which serves the materialistic world order, shall be replaced by a legal system for all Germany.

20.   With the aim of opening to every capable and industrious German the possibility of higher education and of thus obtaining advancement, the state must consider a thorough reconstruction of our national system of education. . . .

21.   The state must see to raising the standard of health in the nation by protecting mothers and infants, prohibiting child labor, increasing bodily efficiency by obligatory gymnastics and sports laid down by law, and by extensive support of clubs engaged in the bodily development of the young.

22.   We demand abolition of a paid army and formation of a national army.

23.   We demand legal warfare against conscious political lying and its dissemination in the press. In order to facilitate creation of a German national press we demand:

a) that all editors of newspapers and their assistants, employing the German language, must be members of the nation;

b) that special permission from the state shall be necessary before non-German newspapers may appear. These are not necessarily printed in the German language;

c) that non-Germans shall be prohibited by law from participation financially in or influencing German newspapers. . . .

It must be forbidden to publish papers which do not conduce to the national welfare. We demand legal prosecution of all tendencies in art and literature of a kind likely to disintegrate our life as a nation, and the suppression of institutions which militate against the requirements above-mentioned.

24.   We demand liberty for all religious denominations in the state, so far as they are not a danger to it and do not militate against the moral feelings of the German race.

The party, as such, stands for positive Christianity, but does not bind itself in the matter of creed to any particular confession. It combats the Jewish-materialist spirit within us and without us. . . .

25.   That all the foregoing may be realized we demand the creation of a strong central power of the state. Unquestioned authority of the politically centralized Parliament over the entire Reich and its organizations; and formation of chambers for classes and occupations for the purpose of carrying out the general laws promulgated by the Reich in the various states of the confederation.

The leaders of the party swear to go straight forward —if necessary to sacrifice their lives—in securing fulfillment of the foregoing points.

— Reading No. 21 —

THE RAPALLO PACT, APRIL 16, 1922 [23]

On April 16, 1922, the German and Soviet representatives to the Genoa Conference drove to Rapallo and signed a treaty. There was nothing sensational about the pact: the two countries merely agreed that they would establish normal diplomatic relations, that neither would ask for reparations, and that they would seek closer economic ties. But the unexpected treaty between the two defeated nations of the war created consternation among the Allies.

✔   ✔   ✔

The German government, represented by Dr. Walther Rathenau, and the government of the Russian Socialist Republic, represented by Tschitscherin, have agreed to the following stipulations:

ARTICLE 1. Both governments agree that the differences between Germany and Russia during the time of war have been resolved on the following matters:

a. The German Reich and the Russian Soviet Republic mutually renunciate compensation for war costs as well as compensation for war damages. . . .

b. Public and private legal relationships broken by the exigencies of war will be regulated on the basis of reciprocity. . . .

c. Germany and Russia mutually agree to restore war prisoners to their countries. . . .

[23] *Deutscher Geschichtskalender*, 1922, I, 254-255. Translated by the editor.

ARTICLE 3. Diplomatic and consular relations between the German Reich and the Soviet government shall be resumed immediately. . . .

ARTICLE 4. Both governments further are agreed that the general legal rights of nationals of one country in the other be reestablished, and that regulations be made for a revival of trade and industrial relations. . . .

ARTICLE 5. Both governments shall regard the industrial needs of their countries in a mutually favorable spirit. . . .

April 16, 1922   RATHENAU   TSCHITSCHERIN

A SONG OF
NATIONALIST YOUTH [24]

The extreme bitterness of nationalist German youth was revealed in one of the songs published in the Social Democrat. *The assassination of Walter Rathenau was foretold in the final lines of the song.*

✦ ✦ ✦

O hero brave whose shot made Gareis fall
And brought deliverance again to all
From all the Socialist swine,
And made the light on our grief shine!
And Rathenau,[25] old Walther,
Shall have a timely halter!
Revenge is near!
Hurrah! is here!

Let us happy be and gay
Smash Wirth's skull until it crack[26]
Happy, happy, tra-la-la,
Soon the Kaiser will be back!
When the Kaiser's home again
We'll cripple Wirth to his great pain;
The rifles shall stutter, tack, tack, tack,
On the Red rascals and the Black.[27]

Beat, beat Wirth, beat him black and blue
Smash his skull till the brains come through;
Shoot down Walter Rathenau
The Goddamned swine of a Jewish sow.

[24] Quoted in Harlan R. Crippen (ed.), *Germany: A Self-Portrait* (London, 1944), p. 162. By permission of Oxford University Press.
[25] Rathenau: Minister of Foreign Affairs.
[26] Dr. Wirth: a leading Catholic politician.
[27] The Socialists were called the "Reds" and the Catholics the "Blacks."

— Reading No. 23 —

THE MURDER OF RATHENAU, JUNE 24, 1922: AN EYEWITNESS ACCOUNT [28]

On June 24, 1922, Walther Rathenau, Germany's foreign minister, was murdered by fanatical members of the Ehrhardt brigade. Rathenau, a distinguished Jewish industrialist, had been working for international cooperation and understanding. An opponent of extreme nationalism, he warned the Germans that they were not members of a superior race. How the assassins overtook Rathenau's car and made their escape was described by an eyewitness, a bricklayer named Krischbin.

↗   ↗   ↗

At about a quarter to eleven two cars came down the Königsallee. In the back of the first car which kept more or less to the middle of the road, a gentleman was sitting. We recognized him at once because the car was open. The second, which was also open, was a dark-gray six-seater, a powerful touring car. Two men in long, brand-new leather coats and helmets were in it. The helmets left their faces exposed and we could see that they were clean shaven. They were not wearing goggles. A great many cars come along the Königsallee in Grunewald, and one doesn't notice each one that passes. However, we all noticed this one, because the magnificent leather coats caught our eyes. The big car overtook the

[28] From the *Vossische Zeitung*. Quoted in Crippen (ed.), *op. cit.*, pp. 175-176. By permission of Oxford University Press.

smaller one, which was driving slowly and almost on the tramlines—no doubt because of the large double curve which is just ahead—and cut in on the right side, so that it forced the little car to go towards the left, almost to our side of the road. When the big car had got about half a length ahead, and the passenger in the other one was hanging out to see if the paint had been scratched, one of the men in the leather coats leant forward, seized a large revolver, whose butt he put in his arm pit, and pointed it at the gentleman in the other car. He did not even need to aim, they were so close. I looked him straight in the eye, so to speak. It was a healthy, open face; what we call "an officer's face." I took cover, because the bullets might have hit us too. The shots came quickly, as quickly as a machine-gun. When the one man had finished shooting, the other one stood up, pulled the pin out of an egg-bomb and threw it into the small car. The gentleman had already collapsed in his seat and was lying on his side. Now the chauffeur stopped, quite near Erdener Street, where there is a rubbish heap, and shouted: "Help! Help!" The big car suddenly leapt forward at full speed and went off down Wallot Street. Meanwhile, the car with the dead man in it stood by the curb. At that moment there was a crash as the bomb exploded. The gentleman in the tonneau was actually lifted up into the air —and the car itself seemed to give a jump. We all ran up and found nine empty cartridge cases on the pavement and the pin from the bomb. Parts of the car had also been blown off. The chauffeur restarted the engine, a girl stepped into the car and supported the gentleman, who was unconscious and probably already dead. Then the car drove back as hard as it could along the way it had come, as far as the police station, which is about thirty yards from the end of the street.

— Reading No. 24 —

DECLARATION OF GERMAN DEFAULT BY THE REPARATIONS COMMISSION, DECEMBER 26, 1922 [29]

Article 231 of the Treaty of Versailles held Germany and her allies responsible for causing "all the loss and damage to which the Allied and Associated Governments and their nationals have been subjected as a consequence of the war imposed upon them by the aggression of Germany and her allies." For the first time in history, a war-guilt clause had been imposed in a peace treaty as a means of justifying the imposition of reparations. Germany was required to pay five billion dollars on account, pending the fixing of a total figure. The Spa Conference (1920) apportioned the prospective indemnity as follows: owed to France, 52 per cent; to the British Empire, 22 per cent; to Italy, 10 per cent; to Belgium, 8 per cent; and to all others, 8 per cent.

By the summer of 1922, Germany was demanding a total moratorium on reparations, insisting that she was unable to meet the enormous outlay. The French, who had carefully counted the telegraph poles that were supposed to be delivered to them by the Germans, demanded that the Reparations Commission declare Germany in default. The commission issued this declaration on De-

[29] Publications of the Reparations Commission, V, *Report on the Work of the Reparations Commission from 1920 to 1922* (London, 1923), pp. 141-142.

cember 26, 1922, thereby providing the legal basis for the occupation of the Ruhr by French, Italian, and Belgian troops in January 1923.

✓   ✓   ✓

On the 20th October, 1922, the French Delegation requested the Commission to declare Germany in default as regards its obligation to furnish timber to France during 1922. Under the above order all the sawn timber (55,000 M) should have been delivered to France before the 30th September, 1922, and the 200,000 telegraph poles ordered by France should have been tendered in uncreosoted condition before the 30th November, 1922. The position on the 30th September, 1922, was as follows:

Category of timber	Amount ordered	Contracts made by German Government	Per cent.	Amount due on 30th Sept.	Amount received in Germany by French Agents at 30th Sept.	Per cent. of the order	Dispatched	Per cent. of the order
Sawn Wood	53,000	54,935	100	55,000	17,417	31.5	15,950	29
Telegraph Poles	200,000	75,694	38	145,000[30]	46,133	23.0	40,047	20

On the 30th November, the deliveries were still considerably in arrears and, on the 1st December, the Commission formally heard the representatives of the German Government on the subject.

On the 26th December, 1922, after careful examination of the German defence, the Commission took the following decision:

"1) It was unanimously decided that Germany had not executed in their entirety the orders passed under Annex IV, Part VIII, of the Treaty of Versailles, for deliveries of timber to France during 1922.

2) It was decided by a majority, the British Delegate voting against this decision, that this non-execution constituted a default by Germany in her obligations within the meaning of paragraph 17 of Annex II." . . .

---

[30] Assuming that the rate of delivery was constant.

— Reading No. 25 —

THE LAST HOURS OF ALBERT LEO SCHLAGETER, MAY 26, 1923 [31]

Albert Leo Schlageter, a German living in the Ruhr during the French occupation, was arrested by the French criminal police, tried for espionage and sabotage, and executed on May 26, 1923. Though undoubtedly guilty, Schlageter was judged a self-sacrificing patriot by the German public. During the Nazi era he was elevated to the position of a martyr. The following description of his last hours portrays him as a national hero.

The writ of execution came to Düsseldorf at 1:30 A.M. At 2 A.M. a pastor and the attorney Sengstock were notified.

Schlageter was awakened. An officer read the writ of execution to him. In front of a French officer Schlageter's face showed no shadow of his inner feelings. He asked that he be allowed to write a few lines to his parents. The handwriting in this last message was firm.

26 May 1923

Dear Parents: Now I am about to take my last steps. I shall make my confession and take communion. Then let us have a joyful reunion in the hereafter.

[31] From Rolf Brandt's biography of Albert Leo Schlageter as quoted in Ernst Forsthoff (ed.), *Deutsche Geschichte seit 1918 in Dokumenten* (Leipzig, 1935), pp. 212-213. Courtesy of Alfred Kröner Verlag. Translated by the editor.

Again my greetings to you all. Father. Mother, Josef, Otto,
Frieda, Ida, Marie, both brothers-in-law, everyone at home.
                                                    Your Albert

The post is sent out. A pastor is led to Schlageter's
cell, so that he can make his last confession and communion.

Schlageter speaks calmly to the French officer: "I
shall not speak with my God in your presence and that
of your soldiers."

The pastor sees the enormously holy seriousness in
the face of the man about to die. He utters a few words,
which convinces the French officer, blushing, to leave
the cell and take his post outside.

Only five minutes were given Schlageter for his last
rites.

The officer came back into the cell and asked him for
his last wish. Schlageter, a bit astonished, stared at him.
But he knew that he must not allow his nerves to break.
He said: "A cigarette."

He took a few puffs, looked at the glowing cigarette,
and threw it to the ground.

With firm step he followed the guard to the automobile standing there.

The French had prepared for the execution in a most
inhuman way. There at the edge of the North Cemetery
was the execution squad. A grave was prepared before
the slope of a quarry. Before it was a strong stake. A
pair of officers, a group of French infantrymen.

The dawn of the young day rose. In the heavens pale
red and then dark red rays, like a wound.

The defenders of Schlageter are at their places. He is
led before them. For a moment he presses his lips together. Then his voice is clear and strong, as if he gave
the command for an order to attack: "*Auf Wie-
dersehen!*"

He calmly allows himself to be led to the execution
spot.

A sergeant directs him to kneel. Schlageter's eyes,
which soon will be denied the sight of this world, begin
to flame again. Never! The Andreas-Hofer song surges
through his mind . . . "I shall die, where I stand." . . .

At that moment several brutish French sergeants bent his knees from behind, so that he sank to the earth. His bound hands were then tied behind him to the stake.

Drums roll. The squad present arms.

Schlageter lifts himself upward.

"Fire!"

The salvo echoes through the morning stillness.

The body sinks down. An under-officer walks to it and places his revolver at the temple.

A revolver shot.

Once again the poor body lifts upward.

Schlageter is finally murdered.

— Reading No. 26 —

FEVER DANCE: BERLIN IN THE DAYS OF INFLATION, 1923 [32]

Berlin during the inflation was a crazy world of hunger, immorality, lust, and sensation. The novelist Leo Lania described the maelstrom in this passage.

Outside the shop windows, the human stream was blocked and swirled about in an eddy. A portrait of the Kaiser was flanked by photos of nude women; the Crown Prince of Meiningen stood cheek by jowl with "documents of feminine beauty." A synthesis of Byzantinism and pornography! A few steps farther down you were invited to behold the "Anatomical Wonder Cabinet." "No children admitted."

[32] Leo Lania, *Today We Are Brothers,* quoted in Crippen (ed.), *op. cit.,* pp. 185-187. By permission of Houghton Mifflin Co.

Prostitutes, pimps, "flying" peddlers. From raincoats to cocaine, from jewels to love—everything on hand, immediate delivery. Boys with painted cheeks and mascara, wearing tight-fitting jackets and pointed shoes; they looked like wax mannequins come to life. Girls, bloated and pale, slipped along the walls like hungry cats.

In the side streets to right and left, police cars stopped. Policemen with shouldered carbines marched by. The windows of the food stores were boarded up. Somewhere in the neighborhood there had been plundering in the afternoon, somewhere there had been shooting. . . .

In those months the people of Berlin did not sleep well. Fear of the uncertain kept them awake, no one could stay at home. It was a mood of paralysis combined with unrest: you were dead tired and at the same time wide awake. All human relations were dissolved, life had become an incomprehensible muddle of numbers, and no one had the strength left to figure out their meaning.

And so everyone rushed to cafés, bars, night-clubs. Every day a new "joint" was opened, and all the places were overflowing. Since one part of the population had sold everything it possessed and another exchanged its dollars only for "tangible goods," a clearance sale in human beings began. As in normal times people sell their labor, strength, or intelligence, today they sold themselves, body and soul. Men who by day profiteered in precious metal or leather traded by night in women and men, love and vice. Everything had its price, and with the dollar at two million marks, the price was very low.

A new industry arose. New professions flourished: gigolos, runners, nude dancers. Secret gambling-clubs were set up in the dining-rooms of high government officials; the widows of generals rented their bedrooms by the hour, middle-class couples publicly exhibited their sex-life for money.

— Reading No. 27 —

THE HITLER-LUDENDORFF *PUTSCH*: MARCH ON THE FELDHERRNHALLE, NOVEMBER 9, 1923 [33]

On November 9, 1923, the morning after Hitler's attempted coup at the Bürgerbräu Keller, *the conspirators decided to march into Munich. When the police fired into the ranks of the marching Nazis, the* putsch *ended in failure. A dramatic account of what happened on the streets of Munich was written by Kurt Ludecke, comrade and friend of Hitler.*

✓   ✓   ✓

The council in the *Bürgerbräu Keller* had become gloomier and gloomier. A hundred plans were discussed and discarded—among them, the desperate coup of storming the Reichswehr barracks before they could be re-enforced. It would have been madness, for the Kampfbund was no match for regular troops with armored cars, light artillery, gas, and all the paraphernalia of war.

Finally Ludendorff's advice prevailed, and it was decided to march into Munich. Counting on a huge popular demonstration in their favor, they hoped that with tens of thousands of burghers marching behind them through the heart of the city the Reichswehr and police would refuse to fire. The situation might be carried, after all, by the strength of the almost unanimous sympathy and

[33] Kurt G. W. Ludecke, *I Knew Hitler* (New York, 1938), pp. 169-171. By permission of Charles Scribner's Sons.

enthusiasm of the people for the "national revolution." Streicher, Esser, and other speakers were sent out to whip up the populace to a favorable response.

In the hour before noon on the 9th of November, about seven thousand men of the Kampfbund, in files of eight abreast, their rifles slung across their backs to proclaim their peaceful intention, marched over the Isar bridge into the inner city, followed by thousands of Nazis and their sympathizers.

Dense cordons of police on the other side of the river were quickly disarmed; some of them even threw away their rifles as they saw Ludendorff and Hitler approach. An ever increasing number of cheering people joined the procession, which wound its way unmolested to the Marienplatz, where most of Munich's citizens had already assembled.

From here a veritable human flood poured down the street toward the Odeonsplatz. Ahead was the Ludwigsstrasse, blocked by Reichswehr. The flood advanced. In its front rank marched Hitler, Ludendorff, and other leaders, directly behind Streicher and a color-bearer with the Hakenkreuz banner. Steadily they went on in the face of the waiting troops.

Suddenly, only a few yards away, Landespolizei—the Bavarian state police—rushed forward from their place of concealment behind the *Feldherrnhalle*, levelled their carbines, and took aim.

A cold-blooded officer, Freiherr von Godin, ordered his platoon to fire on the Nazis. He repeated the order twice, then tore a rifle from the hands of a reluctant soldier. Streicher screamed:

"Ludendorff—don't shoot your General! Hitler and Ludendorff . . . !"

It was too late. A volley rent the air, killing fourteen men in the Nazi ranks.

Ludendorff, erect and unhurt, marched straight ahead and was arrested. Hitler, who had been at Ludendorff's side, walking arm-in-arm with Scheubner-Richter, was dragged to the ground with a dislocated shoulder when the Doctor crumpled under the hail of lead. Hitler's body-guard threw himself on his master, covering him with his body and instinctively thinking, as he later told me: *"Ulrich Graf, jetzt hat's dich doch erwischt!"* He received eleven bullets. Beside him Kurt Neubauer, Ludendorff's faithful valet, who had sprung in front of the General to protect him, lay dead with the upper part of his head ripped away.

At sound of firing, the crowds in the rear wavered and halted. The panic seized the street. In a desperate scramble for safety, every one fled.

The revolution was finished.

Roehm, still holding out in the war ministry, decided that to resist in such a hopeless trap would be to murder his loyal men, two of whom had already been shot. He surrendered and was at once arrested.

Ludendorff was released a few hours later, after pledging his word to hold himself at the disposal of the authorities.

Hitler had been helped to his car and had escaped into the mountains.

When the pain in his shoulder grew unbearable and the gasoline was all but gone, he remembered that they were nearing Uffing, where Hanfstaengl had a country house. By chance Erna Hanfstaengl, Putzi's sister, was at home to admit him. A persistent rumor says that she saved Hitler from suicide in this bitter hour. When, years later, I asked him about it, he answered with great simplicity: "No, that is not true; she did not save me from suicide. Naturally my spirits were very low—the mere presence of a woman may have kept me from the thought of ending my life."

It was there, on November 11, that Hitler was arrested.

— Reading No. 28 —

HITLER'S FINAL SPEECH AT HIS TRIAL FOR TREASON, MARCH 27, 1924 [34]

After the beer-hall putsch, Hitler's trial for treason began before a special court in Munich on February 26, 1924. Lasting for twenty-four days, the trial was reported on the front pages of every German newspaper. For the first time Hitler had an audience outside of Bavaria. He succeeded in turning the proceedings into a triumph. He recovered political initiative by the simple device of assuming full responsibility for the attempt to overthrow the Republic. With these final words he built up the failure of the putsch into one of the great propaganda legends of the movement.

✓   ✓   ✓

I aimed from the first at something a thousand times higher than being a minister. I wanted to become the destroyer of Marxism. I am going to achieve this task, and, if I do, the title of minister will be an absurdity as far as I am concerned. . . .

At one time I believed that perhaps this battle against Marxism could be carried on with the help of the government. In January 1923 I learned that that was just not possible. The hypothesis for the victory of Marxism is not that Germany must be free, but rather Germany will

[34] Quoted in Ernst Forsthoff (ed.), *Deutsche Geschichte seit 1918 in Dokumenten* (Leipzig, 1935), pp. 213-214. Courtesy of Alfred Kröner Verlag. Translated by the editor.

only be free when Marxism is broken. At that time I did not dream that our movement would become great and cover Germany like a flood.

The army that we are building grows from day to day, from hour to hour. Right at this moment I have the proud hope that once the hour strikes these wild troops will merge into battalions, battalions into regiments, regiments into divisions. I have hopes that the old cockade will be lifted from the dirt, that the old colors will be unfurled to flutter again, that expiation will come before the tribunal of God. Then from our bones and from our graves will speak the voice of the only tribunal which has the right to sit in justice over us.

Then, gentlemen, not you will be the ones to deliver the verdict over us, but that verdict will be given by the eternal judgment of history, which will speak out against the accusation that has been made against us. I know what your judgment will be. But that other court will not ask us: Have you committed high treason or not? That court will judge us, the quartermaster-general of the old army, its officers and soldiers, who as Germans wanted only the best for their people and Fatherland, who fought and who were willing to die. You might just as well find us guilty a thousand times, but the goddess of the eternal court of history will smile and tear up the motions of the state's attorney and the judgment of this court: for she finds us not guilty.

— Reading No. 29 —

HITLER DENOUNCES THE TREATY OF VERSAILLES [35]

While in jail at Landsberg after the failure of his putsch of 1923, Hitler wrote a book, Mein Kampf, *which he conceived as a statement of principles and a guide for his followers. This bible of the Nazi faith was a queer mélange of half-truths and nonsense, combined with an almost uncanny insight into the mass mind. Wordy, repetitious, badly written, it reveals Hitler's shrewdness, his aims, methods, and character. In the following passage, Hitler gave little attention to the merits or faults of the system of Versailles, but devoted himself instead to the projection of a basically false image in the conviction that the greater the lie the more people would believe it.*

    1   *1*   *1*

In this period the Festsaal of the Munich Hofbräuhaus assumed an almost sacred significance for us National Socialists. Every week a meeting, almost always in this room, and each time the hall better filled and the people more devoted. Beginning with the "War Guilt," which at that time nobody bothered about, and the "Peace Treaties," nearly everything was taken up that seemed agitationally expedient or ideologically necessary. Especially to the peace treaties themselves the greatest attention was given. What prophecies the young movement kept making to the great masses! And nearly all of which have now been realized! Today it is easy to speak or write about these things. But in those days a public mass meeting, attended, not by bourgeois shopkeepers, but by incited proletarians, and dealing with the topic, "The Peace Treaty of Versailles," was taken as an attack on

[35] Adolf Hitler, *Mein Kampf* (Boston, 1962), trans., H. Manheim, pp. 463-464, 466-468. By permission of Houghton Mifflin Co.

the Republic and a sign of a reactionary if not monarchistic attitude. At the very first sentence containing a criticism of Versailles, you had the stereotyped cry flung at you: "What about Brest-Litovsk?" "And Brest-Litovsk?" The masses roared this again and again, until gradually they grew hoarse or the speaker finally gave up his attempt to convince them. You felt like dashing your head against the wall in despair over such people! They did not want to hear or understand that Versailles was a shame and a disgrace, and not even that this dictated peace was an unprecedented pillaging of our people. The destructive work of the Marxists and the poison of enemy propaganda had deprived the people of any sense. And yet we had not even the right to complain! . . .

In those days I learned something important in a short time, *to strike the weapon of reply out of the enemy's hand myself.* We soon noticed that our opponents, especially their discussion speakers, stepped forward with a definite "repertory" in which constantly recurring objections to our assertions were raised, so that the uniformity of this procedure pointed to a conscious, unified schooling. And that was indeed the case. Here we had an opportunity to become acquainted with the incredible discipline of our adversaries' propaganda, and it is still my pride today to have found the means, not only to render this propaganda ineffective, but in the end to strike its makers with their own weapon. Two years later I was a master of this art.

In every single speech it was important to realize clearly in advance the presumable content and form of the objections to be expected in the discussion, and to pull every one of them apart in the speech itself. Here it was expedient to cite the possible objections ourselves at the outset and demonstrate their untenability; thus, the listener, even if he had come stuffed full of the objections he had been taught, but otherwise with an honest heart, was more easily won over when we disposed of the doubts that had been imprinted on his memory. The stuff that had been drummed into him was automatically refuted and his attention drawn more and more to the speech.

This is the reason why, right after my first lecture on the "Peace Treaty of Versailles," which I had delivered to the troops while still a so-called "educator," I changed the lecture and now spoke of the "Peace Treaties of Brest-Litovsk and Versailles." For after a short time, in fact, in the course of the discussion about this first speech of mine, I was able to ascertain that the people really knew nothing at all about the peace treaty of Brest-Litovsk, but that the adroit propaganda of their parties had succeeded in representing this very treaty as one of the most shameful acts of rape in the world. The persistence with which this lie was presented over and over to the great masses accounted for the fact that millions of Germans regarded the peace treaty of Versailles as nothing more than just retribution for the crime committed by us at Brest-Litovsk, thus viewing any real struggle against Versailles as an injustice and sometimes remaining in the sincerest moral indignation. And this among other things was why the shameless and monstrous word *"reparations"* was able to make itself at home in Germany. This vile hypocrisy really seemed to millions of our incited national comrades an accomplishment of higher justice. Dreadful, but it was so. The best proof of this was offered by the propaganda I initiated against the peace treaty of Versailles, which I introduced by some enlightenment regarding the treaty of Brest-Litovsk. I contrasted the two peace treaties, compared them point for point, showed the actual boundless humanity of the one treaty compared to the inhuman cruelty of the second, and the result was telling. At that time I spoke on this theme at meetings of two thousand people and often I was struck by the glances of three thousand six hundred hostile eyes. And three hours later I had before me a surging mass full of the holiest indignation and boundless wrath. Again a great lie had been torn out of the hearts and brains of a crowd numbering thousands, and a truth implanted in its place.

I considered these two lectures on "The True Causes of the World War" and on "The Peace Treaties of Brest-Litovsk and Versailles," the most important of all, and so I repeated and repeated them dozens of times, always renewing the form, until, on this point at least, a certain clear and unified conception became current among the people from among whom the movement gathered its first members.

— Reading No. 30 —

THE GERMAN REICHSWEHR AND THE WEIMAR REPUBLIC [36]

Despite its specific clauses directed at the revival of German armaments, the Treaty of Versailles was not successful in destroying the tradition of the German army. The German army had played an important role in the structure of the German state throughout the Wars of Liberation (1813-1814), in the Bismarckian Third Reich, and during the Wilhelminian era. It never really fell before Allied blows in World War I. During the Weimar Republic its skeletal organization was retained. Under the able ministration of General Hans von Seeckt the Reichswehr was built into a first-class force and later was merged into the Wehrmacht.

✓   ✓   ✓

The reconstruction of the German army by Seeckt was a great achievement comparable with the reform of the Prussian Army a hundred years before, after the peace of Tilsit; the resemblance between Tilsit and Versailles was a frequent theme of German political writers in those days. But a comparison of the two re-organizations shows that the differences were more important than the resemblances and that Seeckt's achievement was inferior to the outwardly far less successful work of Scharnhorst, Gneisenau, and their collaborators.

Scharnhorst and his helpers had been successful in the main lines of their work because from the beginning

---

[36] Herbert Rosinski, *The German Army* (New York, 1940), pp. 195-200. By permission of *The Infantry Journal,* Washington, D.C., and Harcourt, Brace and World Co., Inc.

the reform of the Prussian Army was for them not an isolated issue, but part of the resurrection of the Prussian state and of the national spirit. In contrast the reorganization of the Reichswehr by Seeckt and the general staff was a temporary and fundamentally unsatisfactory solution because it was an isolated act of the military, not part of a general reconstruction of Republican Germany; it left the army a monolithic block in the totally different world of the Weimar Republic, so that in the state of tension there was certain sooner or later to be open conflict.

The primary responsibility for this rested with the supporters of the Republic; they had the power and therefore the moral obligation to prove the worth of their ideals by giving the German people new forms for their national life. Conditions were by no means so unfavorable for such reconstruction as the recriminations over the loss of the war might lead one to believe. The German people were never nearer to becoming really a nation than under the shock of the breakdown of the Imperial authority and the pressure of common misfortune in those first years after the war; unfortunately in the Republican camp there was not one man capable of rising to the greatness of the hour and of its needs. The long diversion of the Reichstag from political responsibility had done its work only too well; it had eliminated outstanding personalities and left the parties in the hands of mediocrities without statesmanlike views or objects.

Thus instead of leading to a great national union and revival, as in 1807, the defeat in the World War divided the German people still further in sterile recriminations. The Republicans thought only of how to seat themselves in the place vacated by the Imperial government; they were satisfied hastily to patch up a doctrinaire system of parliamentary government, which was unsuitable for the German people, emotionally and politically inexperienced. . . .

The Republic was naturally incapable of incorporating the Reichswehr, an element so foreign to itself. It was unable either to control it or to win its unqualified allegiance, and it was never able to establish normal relations with its armed force, vacillating between distrust and petty pin-pricks on the one hand and vain attempts to conciliate it by yielding to its demands.

One inevitably asks the question whether, in these circumstances, the Reichswehr could not have taken the reconstruction of German political life into his hands, once the Republic had clearly demonstrated its incapacity to do so. That question leads us to consider the share which the Reichswehr took in the unfortunate developments of those years.

If the Republic lacked any real appreciation of the situation, the same was true of the Reichswehr. Seeckt with all his diplomatic qualities was the product of a hundred years of segregation of the army from the political life of the nation. He was an unusually broad-minded soldier, but not a statesman like Scharnhorst. His superiority over Republican and reactionary politicians lay mainly in his ironic scepticism, not in any deeper insight into the needs and possibilities of the time. His secret, as his biographer puts it, was frequently that he had no secret. . . .

This retrospective and negative attitude, however, could not remain forever the political outlook of the Reichswehr. The appeal to the soldier's tradition of an "unpolitical attitude" and self-abnegation had been useful as a temporary makeshift; it was altogether too negative an attitude to serve as a permanent basis for its relations with the political power and the nation itself, for without their support it rightly felt itself to be hanging in the air. The Reichswehr's situation drove Seeckt's successsors in its direction to overstep the narrow limits which he had imposed upon himself and to take a more positive interest and hand in the inner policies of the Republic. Their fault was not that they tried to intervene in the political situation, but that they did so with an inadequate appreciation of the nature and the difficulties of the issues involved. The atmosphere of those years was not calculated to enlighten them. The second half of the Weimar Republic's brief span of life was a period in which only the strongest heads escaped confusion. The pre-war alignments and antagonisms which continued to dominate the first years of the new régime, had gradually become so stale that people in all camps, particularly the

young, were desperately searching for some more in-
spiring direction. Everywhere new political movements,
sects, and creeds began to rise like mushrooms after summer rain, some of them full of sound and creative ideas,
the vast majority of that doctrinaire stamp so attractive
to the German mind. If sober politicians found it difficult at times to keep their heads in this ideological ka-
leidoscope, the leaders of the Reichswehr were hardly to
blame when they failed to distinguish between the possible and the fantastic.

Their confusion was helped by the subtle equivocation
in the formula: "the Reichswehr serves the state, not
the parties." For the state to which the Reichswehr thus
proclaimed its allegiance was not the constitution of the
Weimar Republic nor its concrete government, but the
permanent political substance of the German nation and
its territory. . . .

This tendency to subtle equivocation and underhand
intrigues, contrary to the traditional correctness of the
Prussian officer, was to a large extent the result of the
atmosphere of deception and double-crossing which the
policy of evading the peace treaties had introduced into
the Reichswehr and the Ministry of War. Whatever the
practical results of that policy, there can be no doubt
about its pernicious effect upon the outlook of the German officer. The officer was taught that it was his duty
to deceive not only the enemy, but his own government;
astuteness became not only a virtue, but a duty; it was
inevitable that all borderlines between right and wrong
should become blurred and the only criterion of an action
was whether it fulfilled its purpose.

— Reading No. 31 —

THE DAWES PLAN: STATEMENT OF PRINCIPLES, APRIL 9, 1924 [37]

On April 9, 1924, the committee of experts set up by the Reparations Commission submitted its report, which came to be known as the Dawes Plan. The following excerpt, Section VIII, summarized the "Basic Principles for Germany's Annual Reparations Payments."

✓ ✓ ✓

a) Obligations under the treaty and balancing the Reich budget.

1. The computation of the Reich budget shall not be limited to the expenses of domestic administration.

2. Germany must carry to the limit of her ability her responsibilities for obligations under the treaty.

3. The Reich budget can be brought into balance without consideration for the entire capital debts of Germany.

4. It cannot continue to be brought into balance without annual payments for a considerable time in a definite pattern.

b) Equivalent taxation

1. The domestic obligations of the government have been factually cancelled by the currency collapse.

2. Germany must be charged, therefore, with new obligations equivalent to tax paid by French, English, Italian, and Belgian taxpayers.

[37] Extracted from *Sachverständigen-Gutachten* (Deutsche Verlagsgesellschaft für Politik und Geschichte, Berlin, 1924). Translated by the editor.

3. The treaty recognizes this principle.

4. It is morally sound.

5. It is economically justified in its operation on production costs.

6. This principle is in the fullest measure feasible.

c) The interest of the Allies in Germany's prosperity.

1. The creditors of Germany must share in the progress of Germany's prosperity.

2. This will be reached through an index of prosperity.

d) An important difference exists between the ability of the German people to pay taxes and the ability of Germany to transfer capital to foreign countries.

— Reading No. 32 —

PROCLAMATION BY THE REICH PRESIDENT HINDENBURG TO THE GERMAN PEOPLE, MAY 12, 1925 [38]

In the presidential election of 1925, Field Marshal von Hindenburg called on the Germans to help him in his mission. "I give every German who thinks national my hand. I ask every German: help me to bring about the resurrection of our Fatherland!" On April 26, 1925, Hindenburg was elected to the office of Reich President. On May 12 he issued this proclamation.

✦　　　✦　　　✦

I have taken my new important office. True to my oath, I shall do everything in my power to serve the well

[38] *Deutscher Geschichtskalender*, 1925, I, 22-23. Translated by the editor.

being of the German people, to protect the constitution and the laws, and to exercise justice for every man. In this solemn hour I ask the entire German people to work with me. My office and my efforts do not belong to any single class, nor to any stock or confession, nor to any party, but to all the German people strengthened in all its bones by a hard destiny. I place my trust in Almighty God, who will lead us through the most difficult times to come. I place my trust in the eternal power of life of the German nation. I place my trust in the readiness for sacrifice shown by our people even in the most difficult times. Finally, I place my trust in the great idea of justice, which will eventually win for the German people its worthy place in the world.

My first greetings go to those who have suffered under the sorrows of our time. It goes to all those who try to exist in these hard times. It goes to the entire working population of Germany which has suffered much. It goes to our brothers outside the German borders, who are inextricably bound together with us by ties of blood and culture. It goes especially to the old and sick, who, beset by troubles, go into their dark evening of life. And it goes finally to our German youth, hope of our future.

We shall work together honorably and peacefully to earn the respect and recognition of other peoples, and to free the German name from the unjust stains on its character. From self-respect to respect of the world, from self-trust to trust for others! We want all to work for the benefit of German industry, for German community life, for German culture, for a worthy place in the community of nations.

The nation's leadership reflects the will to unity of the people. Therefore, at this time I extend my hand in spirit to every German. For the sake of our precious dead and for our children and children's children we shall go together on the road to true peace and freedom.

— Reading No. 33 —

THE LOCARNO PACT: TREATY OF MUTUAL GUARANTEE, OCTOBER 16, 1925 [39]

An international conference held at Locarno in October 1925 produced several treaties which represented a triumph for Stresemann, Briand, and Austen Chamberlain, all of whom were working for international cooperation. The most important of these pacts was an agreement confirming the inviolability of the Franco-German and Belgo-German frontiers. The Treaty of Mutual Guarantee between Germany, Belgium, France, Great Britain, and Italy was dated October 16, 1925 and signed on December 1, 1925.

↗   ↗   ↗

The President of the German Reich, His Majesty the King of the Belgians, the President of the French Republic, His Majesty the King of the United Kingdom of Great Britain and Ireland and of the British Dominions beyond the Seas, Emperor of India, and His Majesty the King of Italy;

Anxious to satisfy the desire for security and protection which animates the peoples upon whom fell the scourge of the war of 1914-18;

Taking note of the abrogation of the treaties for the neutralisation of Belgium, and conscious of the necessity of ensuring peace in the area which has so frequently been the scene of European conflicts;

[39] Great Britain, *Parliamentary Papers, 1926.* Vol. XXX. Cmd. 2764.

Animated also with the sincere desire of giving to all the signatory Powers concerned supplementary guarantees within the framework of the Covenant of the League of Nations and the treaties in force between them;

Have determined to conclude a treaty with these objects, and have appointed as their plenipotentiaries: . . .

Who, having communicated their full powers, found in good and due form, have agreed as follows:

ARTICLE 1.   The high contracting parties collectively and severally guarantee, in the manner provided in the following articles, the maintenance of the territorial *status quo* resulting from the frontiers between Germany and Belgium and between Germany and France and the inviolability of the said frontiers as fixed by or in pursuance of the Treaty of Peace signed at Versailles on the 28th June, 1919, and also the observance of the stipulations of Articles 42 and 43 of the said treaty concerning the demilitarised zone.

ARTICLE 2.   Germany and Belgium, and also Germany and France, mutually undertake that they will in no case attack or invade each other or resort to war against each other. . . .

ARTICLE 3.   In view of the undertakings entered into in Article 2 of the present treaty, Germany and Belgium and Germany and France undertake to settle by peaceful means and in the manner laid down herein all questions of every kind which may arise between them and which it may not be possible to settle by the normal methods of diplomacy:

Any question with regard to which the parties are in conflict as to their respective rights shall be submitted to judicial decision, and the parties undertake to comply with such decision. . . .

The detailed arrangements for effecting such peaceful settlement are the subject of special agreements signed this day.

ARTICLE 4.   1.   If one of the high contracting parties alleges that a violation of Article 2 of the present treaty or a breach of Articles 42 or 43 of the Treaty of Versailles has been or is being committed, it shall bring the question at once before the Council of the League of Nations.

2. As soon as the Council of the League of Nations is satisfied that such violation or breach has been committed, it will notify its finding without delay to the Powers signatory of the present treaty, who severally agree that in such case they will each of them come immediately to the assistance of the Power against whom the act complained of is directed.

3. In case of a flagrant violation of Article 2 of the present treaty or of a flagrant breach of Articles 42 or 43, of the Treaty of Versailles by one of the high contracting parties, each of the other contracting parties hereby undertakes immediately to come to the help of the party against whom such a violation or breach has been directed as soon as the said Power has been able to satisfy itself that this violation constitutes an unprovoked act of aggression and that by reason either of the crossing of the frontier or of the outbreak of hostilities or of the assembly of armed forces in the demilitarised zone immediate action is necessary. . . .

ARTICLE 5.   The provisions of Article 3 of the present treaty are placed under the guarantee of the high contracting parties as provided by the following stipulations:

If one of the Powers referred to in Article 3 refuses to submit a dispute to peaceful settlement or to comply with an arbitral or judicial decision and commits a violation of Article 2 of the present treaty or a breach of Articles 42 or 43 of the Treaty of Versailles, the provisions of Article 4 shall apply. . . .

ARTICLE 6.   The provisions of the present treaty do not affect the rights and obligations of the high contracting parties under the Treaty of Versailles or under arrangements supplementary thereto, including the agreements signed in London on the 30th August, 1924.

ARTICLE 7.   The present treaty, which is designed to ensure the maintenance of peace, and is in conformity with the Covenant of the League of Nations, shall not be interpreted as restricting the duty of the League to take whatever action may be deemed wise and effectual to safeguard the peace of the world.

ARTICLE 8.   The present treaty shall be registered at the League of Nations in accordance with the Covenant of the League. It shall remain in force until the Council, acting on a request of one or other of the high contracting parties notified to the other signatory Powers three months in advance, and voting at least by a two-thirds' majority, decides that the League of Nations ensures sufficient protection to the high contracting parties; the treaty shall cease to have effect on the expiration of a period of one year from such decision.

ARTICLE 9. The present treaty shall impose no obligation upon any of the British dominions, or upon India, unless the Government of such dominion, or of India, signifies its acceptance thereof.

ARTICLE 10. The present treaty shall be ratified and the ratifications shall be deposited at Geneva in the archives of the League of Nations as soon as possible.

It shall enter into force as soon as all the ratifications have been deposited and Germany has become a member of the League of Nations.

The present treaty, done in a single copy, will be deposited in the archives of the League of Nations, and the Secretary-General will be requested to transmit certified copies to each of the high contracting parties.

In faith whereof the above-mentioned plenipotentiaries have signed the present treaty.

Done at Locarno, the 16th October, 1925.

> LUTHER
> STRESEMANN
> EMILE VANDERVELDE
> A. BRIAND
> AUSTEN CHAMBERLAIN
> BENITO MUSSOLINI

— Reading No. 34 —

STRESEMANN DEFENDS THE LOCARNO PACT [40]

For his efforts on behalf of the Locarno pact (1925), Gustav Stresemann, the German foreign minister, was strongly criticized by nationalist elements in Germany. The speech, excerpted below, which he made on December 15, 1925, to the Central Association of Provincial Organizations, was designed to meet objections to his foreign policy and to explain the negotiations at Locarno to his countrymen.

The publicity given to our negotiations at Locarno was in certain regards unfortunate. We had decided that our negotiations should be absolutely confidential, which was sensible; no worse nonsense has been talked lately than that about the abolition of secret diplomacy. Every merchant who has some new scheme in view for the coming year does not proclaim it in an announcement in a Berlin newspaper, so that any competitor may see what is coming and take measures accordingly. We perhaps rather overdid the art of secret diplomacy. In the art of saying nothing in our *communiqués,* we really had no rivals. But the Press representatives had to telegraph a thousand lines a day, and they naturally telegraphed a great deal of nonsense. . . . There were stories of mar-

[40] *Gustav Stresemann: His Diaries, Letters, and Papers,* ed. and trans., Eric Sutton (New York, 1935-1937), II, 215-219. By permission of The Macmillan Company and Curtis Brown Ltd.

vellous trips on Lago Maggiore in a boat that was pic-
turesquely named the *Orange Blossom,* and the German
citizen thought to himself that we were having a very
good time indeed. The fact was that on this marvellous
trip we spent more than five hours in the cabin; the first
two and a half hours were occupied in a discussion of
Article 16 of the League Covenant, and the remaining
two and a half hours were taken up with the French
guarantee regarding the Eastern European treaties. I
have never been so tired and done up as I was on that
occasion. And the discussions were so acrimonious that
I wished the minutes of them could have been published
afterwards. . . .

I fancy that most of the attacks upon us would be si-
lenced if the minutes of the meeting were published at
which we discussed German disarmament, and in the
face of Briand, Chamberlain, and Vandervelde, rejected
the charge of War Guilt. I tell you that you are not to
conceive matters as though, under the sunshine of Locarno, we had stumbled into a fresh alliance of friendship. . . .

Let me speak of two groups of questions that were
especially prominent at Locarno. The first was the question of Alsace-Lorraine and Eupen-Malmédy. In Articles
1 and 2 of the treaty is stated what the Powers are to
renounce. They are to renounce war, force, and invasion.
It was laid down in the preamble of the draft—for the
draft was altered three times . . . that the intention of
these treaties is the maintenance of the *status quo* in the
West. This clause was struck out at the suggestion of the
German Delegation, and replaced by the words "maintenance of peace." Our resistance was the fundamental
idea of the whole transaction. The worst of it is that, out
of respect for what was confidential, we cannot give the
proper balance to the situation; it would then become
clear that there was no question of a moral renunciation,
but merely a recognition of the fact, which every sensible
person would admit, that it would to-day be madness to
play with the idea of a war with France.

The second question that came into consideration as
regards the West was that of Eupen-Malmédy. Vandervelde's organ, *Le Peuple,* stated about a fortnight ago

that if Germany would help Belgium over the stabilization of the franc by the recognition of the mark agreement, Belgium might take into consideration the institution of a new plebiscite in Eupen-Malmédy to decide whether it wanted to belong to Germany or Belgium. . . .

As touching Eastern European questions, where the principle of national self-determination has been so grievously violated, I have no notions of decisions to be reached by war. What I have in mind is that when conditions arise which indicate that European peace or the economic consolidation of Europe is threatened by developments in the East, and when it is realized that this entire non-consolidation of Europe appears to have its origin in impossible frontier-lines in the East, that Germany might succeed with her claims, if she had previously effected a political understanding with all the world Powers who would have to decide the matter, and established a common economic interest with her opponents. That, in my opinion, is the only practicable policy. That we should not recognize the frontier in the East, I made clear, to the disgust of the Polish Government, in a public speech before the Foreign Committee of the Reichstag, when I stated that in my opinion no German Government, from the German Nationals to the Communists, would ever recognize this frontier. And I shall never shrink from repeating this declaration.

I see the importance in another connection of this security for peace between ourselves and France. It is true that these are all matters that lie in the future; a nation must not adopt the attitude of a child that writes a list of its wants on Christmas Eve, which contains everything that the child will need for the next fifteen years. The parents would not be in a position to give it all this. In foreign politics I often have the feeling that I am being confronted with such a list, and that it is forgotten that history advances merely step by step, and Nature not by leaps and bounds. . . .

— Reading No. 35 —

THE RUSSO-GERMAN TREATY, APRIL 24, 1926 [41]

On April 24, 1926, Russia and Germany signed a treaty which confirmed and strengthened the relationship begun at Rapallo. Stresemann was willing to sign this pact in order to allay Russian nervousness about the Western orientation of Germany policy. The treaty was received with approval inside Germany, but with suspicion abroad.

✓ ✓ ✓

The German government and the government of the Union of Socialist Soviet Republics, animated by the desire to do all they can to contribute to the maintenance of general peace and convinced that the interest of the peoples of the Union of Socialist Soviet Republics and of Germany demands conscientious and constant collaboration, have come to an agreement to confirm the friendly relations existing between them, and to this end have named two plenipotentiaries: for the German government, the Minister of Foreign Affairs, Gustav Stresemann, and for the Union of Socialist Soviet Republics the Ambassador Extraordinary and Minister Plenipotentiary of the Union of Socialist Soviet Republics, Nicholas Nicolaievich Krestinsky, who, having exchanged their powers, and having found them in good and due order, have decided upon the following provisions:

ARTICLE 1. The Treaty of Rapallo remains the basis

[41] *Europäische Geschichte*, IV, 209-212.

of relations between Germany and the Union of Socialist Soviet Republics. The German government and the government of the Union of Socialist Soviet Republics remain in friendly contact in order to settle amicably all questions of a political and economic nature concerning their two countries.

ARTICLE 2. If one of the contracting parties, despite its peaceful attitude, should be attacked by a third power or by several third powers, the other contracting party shall observe neutrality during the period of the conflict.

ARTICLE 3. If, in the event of a conflict of the nature foreshadowed in Article 2, occurring at a time when either of the two contracting parties is not involved in an armed conflict, a coalition should be formed by third powers with a view to imposing an economic and financial boycott on one of the two contracting parties, the other contracting party will not participate in such a coalition.

ARTICLE 4. This treaty will be ratified, and the ratification documents will be exchanged in Berlin.

The treaty becomes legal with the exchange of ratification documents and shall last for five years. Both parties to this treaty agree that prior to the expiration of this treaty they will come to a mutual understanding about their future relations.

In witness of the above the plenipotentiaries have signed this treaty.

Berlin, April 24, 1926.

(LS) STRESEMANN   (LS) KRESTINSKY

— Reading No. 36 —

GERMANY'S ENTRANCE INTO THE LEAGUE OF NATIONS, SEPTEMBER 8, 1926[42]

The Seventh Assembly of the League of Nations, meeting on September 8, 1926, unanimously elected Germany to a permanent seat on the Council and membership in the Assembly. Two days later Gustav Stresemann, Germany's foreign minister, received a great ovation as he delivered the following speech. It was couched in the most general terms, but obviously Stresemann hoped that the League would remedy what Germans believed to be the injustices of the Treaty of Versailles.

More than six years have passed since the League was founded. A long period of development was thus necessary before the general political situation rendered it possible for Germany to enter the League, and even in the present year great difficulties have had to be overcome before Germany's decision could be supplemented by the unanimous decision of the League. Far be it from me to revive matters which belong to the past. It is rather the task of the present generation to look to the present and to the future. I would only say this, that, although an event such as Germany's entry into the League is the outcome of a long preliminary process of development, yet that very fact constitutes perhaps a

[42] *The League of Nations Official Journal,* Special Supplement No. 44, p. 51, no. 22.

surer guarantee of its permanence and of its fruitful results. . . .

The co-operation of the peoples in the League of Nations must and will lead to just solutions for the moral questions which arise in the conscience of the peoples. The most durable foundation of peace is a policy inspired by mutual understanding and mutual respect between nation and nation.

Even before her entry into the League, Germany endeavored to promote this friendly co-operation. The action which she took and which led to the Pact of Locarno is a proof of this, and as further evidence there are the arbitration treaties which she has concluded with almost all her neighbors. The German Government is resolved to persevere unswervingly in this line of policy and is glad to see that these ideas, which at first met with lively opposition in Germany, are now becoming more and more deeply rooted in the conscience of the German people. Thus the German Government may well speak for the great majority of the German race when it declares that it will wholeheartedly devote itself to the duties devolving upon the League of Nations.

During the past six years the League has already taken in hand a substantial portion of these tasks, and has done most valuable work. The German delegation does not possess the experience which the members here assembled have acquired. We believe, however, that, as regards the new work which lies before us, the subjects dealt with first should be those in which the individual nations can do most by combining in joint institutions. Among other institutions which the League has created, we have in mind the World Court, which is the outcome of efforts made to establish an international legal order. . . .

Germany's relations to the League are not, however, confined exclusively to the possibilities of co-operation in general aims and issues. In many respects the League is the heir and executor of the Treaties of 1919. Out of these Treaties there have arisen in the past, I may say frankly, many differences between the League and Germany. I hope that our co-operation within the League will make it easier in future to discuss these questions. In this respect mutual confidence will, from a political point of

view, be found a greater creative force than anything
else. It would, indeed, be incompatible with the ideals of
the League to group its members according to whether
they are viewed with sympathy or with antipathy by
other Members.

In this connection I reject most emphatically the idea
that the attitude hitherto adopted by Germany in matters concerning the League of Nations has been dictated
by such sympathies or antipathies.

Germany desires to co-operate on the basis of mutual
confidence with all nations represented in the League or
upon the Council.

— Reading No. 37 —

HINDENBURG DEDICATES THE TANNENBERG NATIONAL MONUMENT, SEPTEMBER 18, 1927 [43]

*On September 18, 1927, President von Hindenburg
delivered an address at the dedication of the Tannenberg
national monument in Hohenstein, East Prussia, commemorating the victory there of German armies over the
Russians in the last days of August 1914. This speech expressed deep resentment against the Treaty of Versailles
and its denunciation of the Germans as authors of the
war.*

✔   ✔   ✔

The Tannenberg monument is dedicated above all to
the memory of those who died for the freedom of their

[43] *Deutscher Geschichtskalender, Inland,* July-December, 1927,
p. 9. Translated by the editor.

country. Their memory, as well as the honor of my still-living comrades, obliges me at this time and at this place to declare solemnly:

We, the German people in all strata unanimously reject the charge that Germany is responsible for this greatest of all wars! Neither envy, nor hate, nor lust for conquest gave weapons to our hands. The war was for us the hardest sacrifice of the entire people against a world of enemies. With clean hearts we went to the defense of our Fatherland, and we took the sword with clean hands. Germany is ever ready to substantiate this before impartial judges.

In the countless graves, which give witness to German heroism, lie without distinction the men of all party colors. They are united in their love and loyalty to the common Fatherland. Let this monument shatter all domestic quarrels. It is a place where all who are moved by love for the Fatherland and who treasure German honor above all, can compose their differences. With this wish I open the doors of the Tannenberg national monument.

— Reading No. 38 —

THE YOUNG PLAN:
DR. SCHACHT'S MEMORAN-
DUM, DECEMBER 5, 1929 [44]

*Dr. Hjalmar Horace Greeley Schacht, president of the
Reichsbank, had signed the original text of the Young
Plan in Paris, and thereby alienated his conservative
friends. When Foreign Minister Stresemann later made
a few concessions at the Hague conference, Schacht
seized the opportunity as a pretext for repudiating his
own signature. In a lengthy memorandum, dated December 5, 1929, he expressed his opposition to the Young
Plan. He accused the government of having unnecessarily
accepted changes in the plan to Germany's disadvantage.
He ended with the following definition of his own responsibility. This was, in effect, a declaration of war on
the government. Most sensational of all was the fact that
Schacht gave the memorandum directly to the press, without any consultation with the government. Schacht then
aligned himself with Alfred Hugenberg, leader of the
Nationalists, and Adolf Hitler, the Nazi Fuehrer. A few
months later, he resigned as president of the Reichsbank.*

✓   ✓   ✓

The Young Plan is a treaty structure which I helped,
sincerely and with good will, to build up; and while I
undertook no responsibility for its execution, all of us
who co-operated to create it regarded it as the only pos-

[44] Hjalmar H. G. Schacht, *The End of Reparations,* trans.,
Lewis Gannett (London, 1931), pp. 119-121. Courtesy of
Jonathan Cape, Ltd, and of the Executors of the Hjalmar
Schacht Estate.

sible way to solve the reparations question and by co-operative constructive labour to restore world peace. This Plan is not an accidental piece of literary hack-work, but it expresses the most serious sense of moral responsibility which its authors felt not only to their own people, but to the entire civilized world. We have a right to ask the governments not to endanger this pacific achievement by insisting upon one-sided interests. For my part I must most explicitly refuse to accept responsibility for the institution of the Young Plan, if its programme and provisions are to be neglected as the current proposals and requirements seem to indicate.

The German people have a right to expect the foreign governments to cease their efforts to squeeze out of German industry special payments and sacrifices which go beyond the terms of the Young Plan. These governments must realize that such a dishonest policy would make them responsible, if the Young Plan should be endangered at the very start, and the mobilization of annuities be endangered.

We must ask the German Government not to accept any additional burdens whatever. We must ask it, before it finally accepts the Young Plan, to balance the budgets of the national government, of the states and of the municipalities, and to provide for such a reduction in the burden borne by the German people as will make it possible for German industry to live.

Those who agree with me that the Young Plan is a final instrument of peace, a plan based upon the two assumptions of international co-operation and a flourishing German industry, and that unless these assumptions are fulfilled it will not work—they who agree to this must insist that everything possible be done to make those assumptions real. The world deceives itself if it believes that we can pay millions and milliards beyond the sums assigned us in the Young Plan or that we can sacrifice our property rights. And our own people deceives itself if it believes that with the burdens already imposed by the Young Plan upon our industry, still further sums can be raised.

I do not want to and I will not contribute to such deception.

— Reading No. 39 —

RILKE IS DISILLUSIONED BY THE WEIMAR REPUBLIC [45]

Rainer Maria Rilke (1875-1926), the great German lyric poet, found little to attract him in the German revolution or in the Weimar Republic. Disillusioned about the absence of a real change of heart, he could speak only negatively of the Republic and its chances. The following passage, which Rilke wrote on February 2, 1923, reveals his lack of enthusiasm.

✦   ✦   ✦

For me, as I see things and live through them, perforce in my own way, there is no doubt that it is Germany who is arresting the progress of the world, because she does not know herself. The many-sided and broad nature of my make-up allows me the necessary perspective to see this. Germany in 1918, the hour of collapse, could have shaken and put to shame the whole world by an act of honesty and repentance, by a visible and determined renunciation of her spurious prosperity—in short by a humility which would have been the very essence of her character and dignity and which would have forestalled all the humiliations that could have been imposed on her from without. It was then—so I hoped for a time —that this long-lost trait of humility, so inherent in the charm of Dürer's drawings, would once again have ap-

[45] Rainer Maria Rilke, *Briefe an eine junge Frau*, trans., E. M. Butler, *Rainer Marie Rilke* (Cambridge, 1941), pp. 43 ff.

peared in the strangely one-sided and docile countenance
of Germany. Perhaps there were a few who felt this,
who desired and believed in such a conversion—but now
we begin to perceive that it never took place, and we
are already reaping the harvest. . . .

Germany neglected to re-establish her purest and highest standards, which were based on the most ancient
traditions. Hers was not a complete conversion and
change of heart; she did not acquire that dignity which
springs from the deepest humility; she was concerned
only with salvation in a superficial, hasty, distrustful,
and grasping sense; she wanted to do something and get
away with it, rather than to follow her innermost call,
which was to endure, to overcome and to be ready for
her own miracle. She wanted to persist, and not to alter.

— Reading No. 40 —

THE REVIVAL OF CHAUVINISM

Germany had her share of super-patriots before 1914. There were historians such as Heinrich von Treitschke ("Those who preach the nonsense of eternal peace do not understand Aryan national life"), and militarists such as Friedrich von Bernhardi ("War is a biological necessity"). This type of jingoism died down in the immediate postwar years. Soon revived, it infected reactionary nationalists in the Weimar Republic. In the first excerpt below, a superintendent of schools gave his suggestion for a student's composition on the advantages of war (1927). The second selection extracted from Ewald Banse's Space and People in World War, *reveals the tenor of revived militarism.*

1

DRAFT FOR A STUDENT COMPOSITION ON THE ART OF WAR[46]

I. For the Nation:

1. War is the antidote for the weeds of peace, during which intellectualism takes precedence over idealism and puts everything to sleep.

2. Patriotism is stimulated, and a sacred enthusiasm for the Fatherland is awakened.

3. The triumphant nation obtains a position of power, as well as the prestige and influence it deserves; the honor of the defeated nation is not affected at all if it has defended itself with courage.

[46] K. Dorenwall and A. Vögeler, *Der deutsche Aufsatz in den Hochschulen,* 6th ed. (1927), III, lesson no. 158, p. 362.

4. Peoples learn to know each other better and to respect one another. There is an exchange of ideas, opinions, points of view.

5. Trade finds new routes, often favorable ones.

6. The arts, especially poetry and painting, are given excellent subjects.

II. FOR THE CITIZENS:

1. War gives them the opportunity to develop their talents. Without war the world would have fewer great men.

2. War enables many virtues to assert themselves.

3. Many active persons get the opportunity to make great fortunes.

4. It is sweet to die for the Fatherland. The dead of the enemy live in the memory of the victor.

2

EWALD BANSE CONTRASTS THE WARLIKE MAN
AND THE PACIFIST[47]

The actively warlike man is the man who does not fight to live, but lives to fight. War is his element. His eagle eye is ever on the alert for chances and opportunities of fighting; with his slight frame, which looks as if it were built for cutting through obstacles, he comes down like a wolf on the fold. This born warrior hurls himself without thinking into the mêlée; for him battle is the everlasting, yea, the fulfillment and justification of existence. . . . The essential Nordic original aristocracy of the West, and beyond it, has always been the largest contributor to this class, and has shed its blood on every battlefield of the world. Fighting for fighting's sake, not in defense of hearth and home, is the watchword of this kind. . . .

How utterly different . . . is the peace-loving man, the pacifist! Peace is the only state for which he is fitted and he will do anything to preserve it; he will endure

[47] Ewald Banse, *Germany Prepares for War: A Nazi Theory of "National Defense,"* trans., Alan Harris (London and New York, 1934), pp. 56-57. This is a British version of the original *Raum und Volk im Weltkriege*.

any humiliation, including loss of liberty and even the most severe damage to his pocket, in order to avoid war. His dim, lusterless eye betokens servility (which does not rule out impertinence), his clumsy body is obviously built for toiling and stooping, his movements are slow and deliberate. This type is the born stay-at-home, small-minded, completely flummoxed by the smallest interruption of the normal course of events, looking at the whole world from the standpoint of his little ego and judging it accordingly. . . . The man of peace, be his muscles weak or strong, values honor and renown less than his own little life, which seems too great and important to him. He sets the individual destiny above the destiny of the nation.

— Reading No. 41 —

ALFRED ROSENBERG:
THE MYTH OF THE TWENTIETH CENTURY [48]

Alfred Rosenberg (1893-1946), prophet-laureate of National Socialism, first published The Myth of the Twentieth Century *in 1930. By 1938 the book had run into 142 editions and had sold 713,000 copies. In his work Rosenberg described "the myth of Blood, which under the sign of the swastika, unchained the racial world-revolution." "It is the awakening of the race-soul, which after a long sleep victoriously ends the racial chaos." The book was actually an attack on the democratic essence of the Weimar Republic, and a call to action to adopt in its stead a system of society based on leadership by the élite. Following are brief excerpts which indicate the nature of Rosenberg's philosophy.*

⚡   ⚡   ⚡

A new epoch begins today in which world history will be written anew. The old conceptions of the human past have faded away. . . . A young but ancient feeling of life demands expression, a world view is born. . . .

A new and colorful picture of human and earthly history is beginning to be unveiled today, if we recognize honorably that we must investigate the division between blood and milieu, between blood and blood. But this recognition also includes the knowledge that the struggle

[48] Alfred Rosenberg, *Der Mythus des 20. Jahrhunderts* (39-40th ed., Munich, 1934), pp. 21-23, 116-118, and *passim.*

of bloods and the mysticism of life are not two different things, but one and the same thing. Race is the symbolic expression of a soul. Racial virtue has a value in itself. . . .

Racial history is equivalent to natural history and the mystical soul. The history of the religion of the blood is the story of the rise and fall of peoples, of their heroes and thinkers, their inventors and artists. . . .

A cultured nation will concede to no one the right to judge its creations, by censuring them as good or bad, right or wrong. . . .

Each race has its soul, and each soul belongs to a race. . . . Each race produces in the long run only one supreme ideal. . . . This supreme value demands a definite grouping of the other life-values, which are conditioned by it. It thus determines the character of a race, of a people. . . .

If we tolerate, at the same time, and in the same place, two or more world-outlooks, each one related to a different supreme value, which the *same* people are to share . . . we have sown the germs of a new catastrophe. . . .

History no longer means war of class against class nor of church dogma and dogma, but blood and blood, race and race. . . .

Soul means race, inwardly discerned. Conversely, race is the external aspect of a soul. . . .

Nordic blood represents that mystery which has replaced and overcome the old Sacraments. . . .

The race-bound national soul is the measure of all our thoughts, aspirations of will and deeds, the final criterion of our values. . . .

The foibles of our heroes ought not to be glossed over, but the eternal, the mythical, behind them ought to be intuited and formulated by the questing soul. In this very way there will arise a series of heroic spirits: Odin, Siegfried, Widukind, Frederick II (the Hohenstaufen), Eckehart, von der Vogelweide, Luther, Frederick the Great, Bach, Goethe, Beethoven, Schopenhauer, Bismarck. . . . To serve this new evolution is the mission of school in the coming German *Reich*. It is its most important if not its only task in the decades to come to make the new evaluation self-evident to all Germans.

— Reading No. 42 —

THE GREAT DEPRESSION: THE PRISONERS OF CARLSHAFEN [49]

The Depression of 1929 hit Germany with tremendous force. An accurate picture of these hard times was given by Rudolf Leonhard in a short story titled "A Fairy Tale for Christmas." The scene is Carlshafen, a small town in the west of Germany, whose people were hard hit by the economic collapse. In mid-winter an unemployed man smashed a shop-window. He was arrested and sent to prison. Soon the jail was overwhelmed with unwelcome guests.

✓ ✓ ✓

It was easy enough to arrest the man. He staggered up to the police officer and practically fell into his arms, uttering a shrill, gurgling, and discordant laugh. As he was being taken away he attempted, so far as his handcuffs would permit him, to execute the steps of a clumsy dance.

This was the last of these misdemeanors and the last of the arrests reported by Wentuscheit's paper and the other journals. How people who live outside the pale of society and only very seldom read newspapers reach a common understanding is a mystery. Well, they manage to do so. Soon everyone for dozens and dozens of miles round knew that something queer was going on in Carlshafen and knew what that something was. How many

[49] Rudolf Leonhard, "A Fairy Tale of Christmas," trans., James Cleugh, quoted in Harlan R. Crippen (ed.), *Germany: A Self-Portrait* (London, 1944), pp. 249-250. By permission of Oxford University Press.

thousands, hundreds of thousands, are to be found lying about, tramping and living their whole lives on the
main roads of Germany since the crisis set in and the
terrible period of destitution began throughout the
country?

These men came, in their hundreds, in their thousands,
and in their tens of thousands. They came from Boden-
werder, from Münden, from Cassel, from Hanover and
Hildesheim, from the Eifel and Sigerland districts. They
came from streets and asylums and ditches and empty,
draught-filled barns. They came, all on foot, in a shuf-
fling, lounging, irresistible flood. The next evening there
was not a single unbroken pane of glass in Carlshafen,
and that in midwinter. Winter, moreover, set in very
severely, particularly severely, that year.

The Carlshafen police were not sufficiently numerous
to deal with the situation. Reinforcements were tele-
phoned for. The magistrate had his hands chock-a-block
with cases. The prison was crammed to overflowing.
More prisons were improvised in the damp, empty warehouses. But even these were not enough. In spite of the
fact that these 'voluntary' prisoners were only given thin
turnip soap and a little bread, just like the 'involuntary'
ones, something like famine became imminent in Carlshafen. The prisoners preferred the turnip soup, which
was at least warm, to nothing at all. They gobbled up
and sucked in greedily everything they were given.

What was to be done? Was there to be overcrowding
and underfeeding, a shortage of accommodation and a
shortage of victuals, just at Christmas time, in the midst
of this severe winter? Meanwhile more and more men
kept arriving and no windows remained to be smashed
in the whole of Carlshafen.

An attempt was made to get the invaders out of the
town. But it did not succeed. No sooner was one of them
driven from the corner-post he was sitting on or from
the wall against which he leant, than he simply walked
round the square and came back ten minutes later, if it
was the inner square, or a quarter of an hour later if it
was the outer, to his old position and sat down or leant
against his wall as before. No one knew how many there
were of them. They completely filled the streets, which in

Carlshafen are simply the long, open corridors surrounding the sides of the squares. They stood or lay about in the streets as if they had taken root there. The streets were gray, their faces were gray, and even the hair on the heads and the stubble on the cheeks of the youngest there were gray with dust and their adversity. They sat or lay on the pavements or in the roadway and gravely shared out scraps of newspaper among themselves. Wentuscheit's article was printed in more than one of the papers that changed hands. . . .

The upshot of the various businesslike, earnest, acrimonious, angry, excited, and clamorous telephone conversations between the judicial and administrative authorities, between the local and provincial bodies, was a determination to keep the situation in hand, not arrest anybody and empty the prisons so far as possible.

Accordingly, those who were sitting, lying, squatting and standing in the streets suddenly saw the doors of the prison and the warehouses, after certain slight and not very intelligible noises behind the walls, open all together. They perceived that people devilishly like themselves were being urged to leave the buildings. They were being urged in every sense of the word. For they were being thrust out of the gates at first gently, then less gently and finally with positive violence. These were the men who had first been arrested and whose brief sentence had now expired. And they didn't want to go. In the end they were relentlessly flung out of the prison. At once they were swallowed up and sucked in by the multitudes of the rest, just as if they had never been separated.

— Reading No. 43 —

A GOEBBELS' PROPAGANDA PAMPHLET, 1930 [50]

Hitler's drive to power was sparked by an ingenious propaganda campaign directed by Dr. Joseph Goebbels (1895-1945). A gnome-like little man with a club foot, Goebbels was born in a small Rhineland town, studied at several universities, and became drawn to a nihilistic philosophy. In 1922, after hearing Hitler speak, he joined the National Socialist party. Promoted to its chief propagandist, he made a study of American advertising and promotion techniques and applied them to Germany. He transformed political rallies into colorful spectacles with music, flags, and parades. His recurrent theme was that Hitler was the superman destined to save Germany. His Machiavellian adroitness is revealed in this pamphlet written in 1930 when the Nazis were driving to political power.

WHY ARE WE NATIONALISTS?

We are NATIONALISTS because we see in the NATION the only possibility for the protection and the furtherance of our existence.

The NATION is the organic bond of a people for the protection and defense of their lives. He is nationally minded who understands this IN WORD AND IN DEED.

[50] Adapted from Joseph Paul Goebbels, *Die verfluchten Hakenkreuzler. Etwas zum Nachdenken* (Munich, 1930), pp. 1-28, *passim.* Translated by the editor.

Today, in GERMANY, NATIONALISM has degenerated into BOURGEOIS PATRIOTISM, and its power exhausts itself in tilting at windmills. It says GERMANY and means MONARCHY. It proclaims FREEDOM and means BLACK-WHITE-RED.

WE ARE NATIONALISTS BECAUSE WE, AS GERMANS, LOVE GERMANY. And because we love Germany, we demand the protection of its national spirit and we battle against its destroyers.

WHY ARE WE SOCIALISTS?

We are SOCIALISTS because we see in SOCIALISM the only possibility for maintaining our racial existence and through it the reconquest of our political freedom and the rebirth of the German state. SOCIALISM has its peculiar form first of all through its comradeship in arms with the forward-driving energy of a newly awakened nationalism. Without nationalism it is nothing, a phantom, a theory, a vision of air, a book. With it, it is everything, THE FUTURE, FREEDOM, FATHERLAND!

It was a sin of the liberal bourgeoisie to overlook THE STATE-BUILDING POWER OF SOCIALISM. It was the sin of MARXISM to degrade SOCIALISM to a system of MONEY AND STOMACH.

SOCIALISM IS POSSIBLE ONLY IN A STATE WHICH IS FREE INSIDE AND OUTSIDE.

DOWN WITH POLITICAL BOURGEOIS SENTIMENT: FOR REAL NATIONALISM!

DOWN WITH MARXISM: FOR TRUE SOCIALISM!

UP WITH THE STAMP OF THE FIRST GERMAN NATIONAL SOCIALIST STATE!

AT THE FRONT THE NATIONAL SOCIALIST GERMAN WORKERS PARTY! . . .

WHY DO WE OPPOSE THE JEWS?

We are ENEMIES OF THE JEWS, because we are fighters for the freedom of the German people. THE JEW IS THE CAUSE AND THE BENEFICIARY OF OUR MISERY. He has used the social difficulties of the broad masses of our people to deepen the unholy split between Right and Left among our people. He has made two halves of Germany. He is the real cause for our loss of the Great War.

The Jew has no interest in the solution of Germany's fateful problems. He CANNOT have any. FOR HE LIVES ON THE FACT THAT THERE HAS BEEN NO SOLUTION. If we would make the German people a unified community and give them freedom before the world, then the Jew can have no place among us. He has the best trumps in his hands when a people lives in inner and outer slavery. THE JEW IS RESPONSIBLE FOR OUR MISERY AND HE LIVES ON IT.

That is the reason why we, AS NATIONALISTS and AS SOCIALISTS, oppose the Jew. HE HAS CORRUPTED OUR RACE, FOULED OUR MORALS, UNDERMINED OUR CUSTOMS, AND BROKEN OUR POWER.

THE JEW IS THE PLASTIC DEMON OF THE DECLINE OF MANKIND.

WE ARE ENEMIES OF THE JEWS BECAUSE WE BELONG TO THE GERMAN PEOPLE. THE JEW IS OUR GREATEST MISFORTUNE.

It is not true that we eat a Jew every morning at breakfast.

It is true, however, that he SLOWLY BUT SURELY ROBS US OF EVERYTHING WE OWN.

THAT WILL STOP, AS SURELY AS WE ARE GERMANS.

— Reading No. 44 —

THE HORST WESSEL SONG [51]

*Propaganda minister Goebbels considered it important
to have a revolutionary song "whose chords would ring
out on the barricades of freedom." He found his man
in Horst Wessel, a young Nazi storm-trooper. The student had broken with his father, a Protestant military
chaplain, and led the life of a bohemian in a slum section of Berlin with a girl who had once been a prostitute.
In February 1930, an enemy gang invaded Wessel's room
and killed him. Goebbels, calling Wessel a Nazi martyr,
elevated him to the level of a national hero. Wessel left
behind him a marching song which included the party's
most familiar slogans set to music borrowed from various tunes. The "Horst Wessel Song" became the Nazi's
official ballad in the drive for power, and, later, was
adopted as a second national anthem. Following are the
first three stanzas.*

1.

*Die Fahne hoch, die Reihen dicht geschlossen!
S.A. marschiert mit ruhig festem Schritt.
Kam'raden, die Rotfront und Reaktion erschossen,
Marschieren im Geist in unsern Reihen mit.*

2.

*Die Strasse frei den braunen Bataillonen!
Die Strasse frei dem Sturmabteilungsmann!
Es schaun aufs Hakenkreuz voll Hoffnung schon Mil-
lionen,
Der Tag für Freiheit und für Brot bricht an.*

[51] Translated by the editor.

3.

Zum letzten Mal wird nun Appell geblasen!
Zum Kampfe stehn wir alle schon bereit.
Bald flattern Hitlerfahnen über allen Strassen,
Die Knechtschaft dauert nur noch kurze Zeit! . . .

1.

Hold high the banner! Close the hard ranks serried!
S.A. marches on with sturdy stride.
Comrades, by Red Front and Reaction killed, are buried,
But march with us in image at our side.

2.

Gang way! Gang way! now for the Brown battalions!
For the Storm Trooper clear roads o'er the land!
The Swastika gives hope to our entranced millions,
The day for freedom and for bread's at hand.

3.

The trumpet blows its shrill and final blast!
Prepared for war and battle here we stand.
Soon Hitler's banners will wave unchecked at last,
The end of German slav'ry in our land! . . .

— Reading No. 45 —

CLEMENCEAU WARNS OF GERMANY REARMING, 1930 [52]

Georges Clemenceau (1841-1929), wartime premier of France, was called the "Tiger," because of his political vehemence. During World War I he fired the soul of France and steeled her will. At the Versailles conference he insisted upon a harsh peace for the Germans. After the war, anticipating the resurgence of German military power, he fought bitterly against its revival. He wanted no German "equality" in armaments. "When I die," he said, "bury me standing up, marching toward Germany!" His opposition to German rearmament was expressed in his book, Grandeur and Misery of Victory *(1930).*

✓   ✓   ✓

What we are doing, then, if not proceeding, article by article, to restore Germany's power, which, by a truly miraculous exercise of will, after its complete collapse during the War, is about to be built up again in the retrograde peace, which is surrendering, stage by stage, everything that human justice has gained by our victory. After the restoration of Germany's moral prestige by a lie we have the upsetting of the financial reparations by the progressive series of mutilations of the Treaty down to the payment of the so-called debts to America!

[52] Georges Clemenceau, *Grandeur and Misery of Victory*, trans., F. M. Atkinson (New York, 1930), pp. 384-385, 389-392. By permission of Harcourt, Brace and World Inc., and the Estate of Georges Clemenceau.

Finally, when this account is settled, or simply opened for the first cut of the final, fatal wound, it will be represented to us that the fabric of European justice according to the Treaty of Versailles has on all sides caused nothing but social disturbance and recriminations leading to outbreaks of violence. That will be the day toward which Germany has been ceaselessly striving since the Treaty of Versailles.

What forces are at the disposal of the new nations of Central Europe? What help will they afford us, and what support are we in a position to offer them? All the problems raised by the German aggression of 1914 will have to be dealt with at one and the same time. Germany, having regained her strength, will have inevitably bargained for arrangements from which her concern to isolate France will not be excluded. . . .

If Germany, still obsessed by her traditional militarism, persists in her *Deutschland über alles,* well—let the die be cast. We shall take up the atrocious War again at the point where we left it off. We must have the courage to prepare for it, instead of frittering away our strength in lies that no one believes, from conference to conference.

If Germany desires to prepare herself to live in peace let her say it, LET HER PROVE IT, and we shall not need the Geneva Chinese to reconcile us. I simply entreat Providence to preserve us from the talkers, and find us, if we still have any, vigilant men. Citizens of the new *régime* of European justice, your day has come. Fashion your destiny yourselves. . . .

The notion of an extravagant act of generosity toward the defeated nation with a view to founding a lasting peace was well calculated to arouse our hopes. But could we really be asked to embark on such a venture without having first assured ourselves of the attitude of a partner who had displayed sentiments with regard to us very far removed from those it was our sincere purpose to awake in him? His acts of folly spring from the innate weakness of the German, which hands him over to the violences of what I shall call the primitive manifestations of human animality.

When I am told that a policy of concessions, more or

less happily graduated, is going to regain for us the goodwill of our former enemies I can only be glad to hear it,
for I desire nothing so much as a state of stable equilib-
rium in Europe. But I must be able to perceive some
sign of a favorable response to the goodwill that I am
asked to manifest. Judge then of my surprise when I discover that *Germany goes on arming and France disarming.* The position is that the most scientific prepara-
tions for war are being carried out on the other side of
the frontier. With us frontiers lie open, armaments are
insufficient, effectives are well below the numbers recognized as necessary, while on the other side a feverish life
of reconstruction is developing and reorganizing, by the
adaptation of fresh material, every department of their
war equipment as well as their means of transport. Never
was work more generally agreed upon. No complaining.
No resistance. Goodwill. Universal enthusiasm the moment the word "war" is thrown to the passions of the
mob, and no sign of a Franco-German reconciliation.

"Germany is arming and France disarming": that is the
decisive feature of this moment of history when the two
states of mind confront one another in such stark brutality that I defy any sane man to cast doubt on the evidence.

— Reading No. 46 —

HITLER'S DÜSSELDORF SPEECH TO THE RHINELAND INDUSTRIALISTS, JANUARY 27, 1932 [53]

On January 27, 1932, Hitler, on invitation of Fritz Thyssen, addressed the Industry Club of Düsseldorf, composed of Rhenish-Westphalian industrialists. In a harangue brilliantly tailored to the views of his audience, Hitler repeated each of his stock ideas. A historic speech, lasting two and a half hours, it made a deep impression on the assembled industrialists, and won for Hitler their financial support. The condensation below summarizes the salient points of this speech.

The dominant consideration in politics today should not be foreign relations. I regard it as of the first importance that we break down the view that our destiny is conditioned by world events. The most important factor in national life is the inner worth of a people and its spirit. In Germany, this inner worth has been undermined by the false values of democracy and the supremacy of mere numbers in opposition to the creative principle of individual personality.

Private property can only be justified on the ground that men's achievements in the economic field are unequal. But it is absurd to construct economic life on achievement of personality, while in political life this authority is denied, and thrust in its place is the law of the greatest number—democracy.

[53] Condensed from the official German version, January 27, 1932. Translated by the editor.

Communism is more than just a mob storming about in our German streets. It is taking over the entire Asiatic world. Unemployment is driving millions of Germans to look on Communism as the logical theoretical counterpart of their actual economic situation. This is the heart of the German problem. We cannot cure this state of affairs by emergency decrees.

There can only be one basic solution—the realization that a flourishing economic life must be protected by a flourishing, powerful state. Behind this economic life must stand the determined political will of the nation ready to strike, and strike hard.

This same is true of foreign policy. The Treaty of Versailles is the result of our own inner confusion. It is no good appealing for national unity and sacrifice when only fifty per cent of the people are ready to fight for the national colors.

Today we stand at a turning point in Germany's destiny. Either we shall succeed in working out a body-politic as hard as iron from this conglomeration of parties, or Germany will fall into final ruin. Today no one can escape the obligation to complete the regeneration of the German body-politic. Every one must show his personal sympathy, and every one must take his place in the common effort. I speak to you today not to ask for your votes or to induce you to do this or that for the party. No, I am here to present a point of view. I am convinced that victory for this point of view is the only starting-point for German recovery.

Remember that it means sacrifice when today hundreds of thousands of S.A. and S.S. men mount their trucks, protect meetings, undertake marches, sacrifice themselves day and night, and then return in the grey dawn to workshop and factory, or, as jobless, take the pittance of a dole. It means sacrifice when these little men spend all their money to buy uniforms, shirts, badges, and even pay their own fares.

But there is in all this the strength of an ideal—a great ideal. If the entire German nation today had this idealism, Germany would look far different in the eyes of the world than she does now!

— Reading No. 47 —

THE HINDENBURG-HITLER
INTERVIEW, AUGUST 13, 1932 [54]

On the afternoon of August 13, 1932, Hindenburg re-
ceived Hitler in the president's palace. The interview, a
chilly affair, lasted only fifteen minutes. When Hinden-
burg offered Hitler a post in a cabinet, Hitler curtly
turned it down. When Hitler demanded the chancellor-
ship, Hindenburg refused. The president admonished
Hitler to conduct himself properly. The following ver-
sion of the interview is taken from the Völkischer Beobachter, *the official Nazi newspaper.*

On Saturday, [August 13] the Führer was received by
Reich Chancellor von Papen, who invited him to be in-
terviewed by Reich President von Hindenburg. To the
question as to whether he and the Party were ready to
enter the von Papen cabinet, the *Führer* declared:

> We are ready and willing to take over full responsibility
> for German political policies in every form, provided that
> that means unequivocal leadership of the government. If
> that is not the case, then the National Socialist Movement
> can accept neither power nor responsibility. Specifically, it
> declines entrance into a cabinet headed by von Papen.

Since the Reich President, however, declined to en-
trust the National Socialist movement, even though it is

[54] *Völkischer Beobachter*, August 17, 1932. Translated by the
editor.

the strongest party in the country, with control of the government, the negotiations were broken off as fruitless.

Appropriate measures for the continuation of the struggle of the National Socialist movement will take place in conferences led by the Führer in the next several weeks.

The Führer left Berlin on Saturday.

— Reading No. 48 —

RESIGNATION OF THE SCHLEICHER CABINET, JANUARY 28, 1933[55]

Desperately holding on to power in the face of Hitler's drive for the chancellorship, General Schleicher asked Hindenburg to dissolve the Reichstag, which was due to reconvene on January 31, 1933. Schleicher's solution was to be a military dictatorship. To Schleicher's dismay, Hindenburg refused to grant him this authority. Realizing that the end was at hand, Schleicher resigned on January 28, 1933.

Berlin 28 January (Telegram)

Reich Chancellor von Schleicher today informed the Reich President about the situation. He declared that the present Reich government would be unable to defend itself vis-à-vis the Reichstag if it did not obtain in advance the power to dissolve parliament. Reich President von Hindenburg stated that he could not grant this proposal because of current conditions. Reich Chancellor von Schleicher then announced the resignation of the government since it had lost the confidence of the Reich President and therefore could not continue in office. The Reich President thanked the Reich Chancellor and his colleagues in the cabinet for their services in difficult times.

Reich President von Hindenburg summoned former Reich Chancellor von Papen and requested him to clarify the political situation and to suggest possible procedures.

[55] *Kölnische Zeitung,* January 28, 1933, evening edition. Translated by the editor.

— Reading No. 49 —

HITLER NAMED CHANCELLOR, JANUARY 30, 1933 [56]

On January 30, 1933, promptly at noon, Hindenburg received Hitler and Papen. Papen informed Hindenburg that Hitler had succeeded in forming a government of national concentration. The oath of office was then administered: Hitler promised to uphold the constitution and rule by legal means. The Weimar Republic was dead. That night Hindenburg and Hitler, at a window of the Reich chancellery, looked on as a great torchlight procession filed past.

At noon today the Reich President received the *Führer* of the National Socialist Party, Hitler, as well as former Reich Chancellor von Papen in an extended interview. The Reich President named Herr Hitler to the office of Reich Chancellor. At Hitler's nomination the following cabinet was named:

Former Reich Chancellor von Papen, Vice Reich Chancellor and Reich Commissioner for Prussia
Baron von Neurath, Reich Minister for Foreign Affairs
State Minister Dr. Frick, Reich Minister of the Interior
General Lieutenant von Blomberg, Reich Minister of War
Count Schwerin von Krosigk, Reich Minister of Finance
Privy Finance Councillor Hugenberg, Reich Minister of

[56] *Kölnische Zeitung*, January 30, 1933, evening edition. Translated by the editor.

Economics and Agriculture

Franz Seldte, Reich Minister of Labor

Baron von Eltz-Rübenbach, Reich Postal and Communications Minister,

and

Reichstag President Göring, Reich Minister without Portfolio and at the same time Reich Commissioner for the *Luftwaffe*. Reich Minister Göring was entrusted with the task of supervising the business of the Prussian Ministry of the Interior.

Reich Commissioner for Employment Opportunities Gereke was retained in his post.

Nominations for the Reich Ministry of Justice are postponed for the moment. The Reich Chancellor will begin discussions today with the Center Party and the Bavarian People's Party. The first cabinet session will take place today at 5:00 P.M.

— Reading No. 50 —

LAW FOR THE REORGANIZATION OF THE REICH, JANUARY 30, 1934 [57]

Hitler obtained the chancellorship through legal methods on January 30, 1933. During the next year, he issued a series of decrees and laws calling for coordination of every phase of the nation's life: The Law to Combat the Crisis of People and State (March 24, 1933); The Law for the Restoration of the Civil Service (April 7, 1933); First Decree for the Execution of the Law for Restoration

[57] Quoted in Henri Lichtenberger, *The Third Reich* (New York, 1937), p. 305. Translated by Koppel S. Pinson.

*of the Civil Service (April 11, 1933); Decree Concern-
ing the Tasks of the Ministry for Public Enlightenment
and Propaganda (June 30, 1933); Law Concerning the
Perpetuation of Inheritable Diseases (July 14, 1933);
Hereditary Farm Laws (September 29, 1933); and Law
to Regulate National Labor (January 20, 1934).*

*On January 30, 1934, precisely one year after becom-
ing chancellor, Hitler issued a basic Law for the Reorganization of the Reich, the text of which follows.*

✓   ✓   ✓

ARTICLE 1.   The popular assemblies of the states are
hereby abolished.

ARTICLE 2.   (1) The sovereign rights of the states are
hereby transferred to the Reich.

(2) The governments of the states are
subordinate to the Reich government.

ARTICLE 3.   The Federal Governors of the states are
subject to the supervision of the Reich Minister of Interior.

ARTICLE 4.   The Reich government may lay down
new constitutional laws.

ARTICLE 5.   The Reich Minister of Interior is to
issue the necessary legal decrees and administrative
measures for the carrying out of this law.

ARTICLE 6.   This law becomes effective on the day
it is promulgated.

APPENDIX

REICH CHANCELLORS OF THE WEIMAR REPUBLIC, 1919-1933

1919, Feb.—1919, June
Philipp Scheidemann
1919, June—1920, Mar.
Gustav Bauer
1920, Mar.—1920, June
Hermann Müller
1920, June—1921, May
  Konstantin Fehrenbach
1921, May—1922, Nov.
Joseph Wirth
1922, Nov.—1923, Aug.
Wilhelm Cuno
1923, Aug.—1923, Nov.
Gustav Stresemann
1923, Nov.—1925, Jan.
Wilhelm Marx
1925, Jan.—1926, May
Hans Luther
1926, May—1928, June
Wilhelm Marx
1928, June—1930, Mar.
Hermann Müller
1930, Mar.—1932, May
Heinrich Brüning
1932, May—1932, Nov.
Franz von Papen
1932, Dec.—1933, Jan.
Kurt von Schleicher
1933, Jan. 30
Adolf Hitler

RECOMMENDED READING

Angell, James W., *Recovery of Germany* (New Haven, 1929).

Barth, Emil, *Aus dem Werkstatt der deutschen Revolution* (Berlin, 1919).

Bergsträsser, L., *Geschichte der politischen Parteien in Deutschland* (7th ed., Munich, 1952).

Bernhard, George, *Die deutsche Tragödie* (Prague, 1933).

Bernstein, Eduard, *Die deutsche Revolution* (Berlin, 1921). Uncompleted.

Blachly, Frederick F., and Miriam E. Oatman, *The Government and Administration of Germany* (Baltimore, 1928).

Bouton, Stephen Miles, *And the Kaiser Abdicates: The German Revolution, November, 1918—August, 1919* (rev. ed., New Haven, 1921).

Bracher, Karl D., *Die Auflösung der Weimarer Republik* (2nd ed. Stuttgart, 1957).

Braun, Otto, *Von Weimar zu Hitler* (New York, 1940).

Clark, Robert T., *The Fall of the German Republic* (London, 1935).

Coar, John F., *The Old and the New Germany* (New York, 1924).

Ebert, Friedrich, *Schriften, Aufzeichnungen, Reden,* ed. Friedrich Ebert, Jr., (2 vols., Dresden, 1926).

Eyck, Erich, *A History of the Weimar Republic* (2 vols., Cambridge, Mass., 1962, 1964).

Forsthoff, Ernst, *Deutsche Geschichte seit 1918 in Dokumenten* (Leipzig, 1935).

Friedensberg, Ferdinand, *Die Weimarer Republik* (Berlin, 1946).

Gatzke, Hans W., *Stresemann and the Rearmament of Germany* (Baltimore, 1954).

Gerschenkron, Alexander, *Bread and Democracy in Germany* (Berkeley, 1943).

Gooch, George P., *Germany* (London and New York, 1925).

Gordon, Harold J., *The Reichswehr and the German Republic, 1919-1926* (Princeton, 1957).

Gumbel, E. J., *Verräter verfallen der Feme. Opfer, Mörder, Richter* (Berlin, 1929).

218

Halperin, S. William, *Germany Tried Democracy: A Political History of the Reich from 1918 to 1932* (New York, 1946). Norton Library edition, 1965.

Harms, Bernhard, *Zehn Jahre deutsche Geschichte, 1918-1928* (2nd ed., Berlin, 1928).

Heiden, Konrad, *A History of National Socialism* (New York, 1935).

Hoover, Calvin D., *Germany Enters the Third Reich* (New York, 1933).

Jordan, W. M., *Great Britain, France and the German Problem, 1918-1939* (New York, 1944).

Kessler, Harry, Graf von, *Walter Rathenau*, trans., W. D. Robson-Scott and Lawrence Hyde (London, 1929).

Klemperer, Klemens von, *Germany's New Conservatism: Its History and Dilemma in the Twentieth Century* (Princeton, 1957).

Kraus, Herbert, *Germany in Transition* (Chicago, 1924).

Luehr, Elmer, *New German Republic* (New York, 1929).

Lutz, Robert H., *The German Revolution, 1918-1919* (Stanford, 1922).

Max von Baden, Prince, *Memoirs,* trans., W. M. Calder and C. W. H. Sutton (2 vols., New York, 1928).

Mommsen, Wilhelm, and Franz Günther, *Deutsche Parteiprogramme, 1918-1930* (Leipzig, 1931).

Müller, Richard, *Vom Kaiserreich zur Republik* (Berlin, 1928).

Neumann, Sigmund, *Die deutschen Parteien* (Berlin, 1932).

Noske, Gustave, *Von Kiel bis Kapp: Zur Geschichte der deutschen Revolution* (Berlin, 1920).

Pinson, Koppel L., *Modern Germany* (New York, 1954).

Quigley, Hugh and R. T. Clark, *Republican Germany* (New York, 1928).

Röpke, Wilhelm, *German Commercial Policy* (London, 1934).

Rosenberg, Arthur, *A History of the German Republic* (London, 1936).

Salomon, Ernst von, *Das Buch vom deutschen Freikorpskämpfer* (Berlin, 1938).

Scheidemann, Philipp, *Memoirs: The Making of the New Germany* (2 vols., New York, 1929).

Scheele, Godfrey, *The Weimar Republic: Overture to the Third Reich* (London, 1946).

Stampfer, Friedrich, *Die vierzehn Jahre der ersten deutschen Republik* (Karlsbad, 1936).

Stresemann, Gustav, *His Diaries, Letters, and Papers,* ed. and trans., Eric Sutton (3 vols., London, 1935-40).

Volkmann, E. O., *Revolution über Deutschland* (Oldenburg, 1930).

Waite, Robert G., *Vanguard of Nazism: The Free Corps Movement in Post-War Germany, 1918-1923* (Cambridge, Mass., 1952).

Wheeler, Bennett, John W., *The Nemesis of Power: The German Army in Politics, 1918-1945* (London and New York, 1954).

———, *Twenty Years of German History, 1914-1934* (New York, 1936).

INDEX

VAN NOSTRAND ANVIL BOOKS already published